M. O. EDWARDS

BROTHERS IN ARMS

M. O. EDWARDS

BROTHERS IN ARMS

by

THOMAS NAPIER TURNBULL

PURITAN PRESS

FOREWORD

TO youthful members of the Apostolic fellowship throughout the British Isles and to many in the vast Apostolic
family overseas the subjects of this biography—Pastors D. P.
and W. J. Williams—may have become vague and shadowy.
Young people have always listened eagerly as older folks
recalled and recounted their personal reminiscences of the
early days when, despite strong opposition and bitter persecution, the Work grew and prospered under the evident
blessing of God.

But over half a century of war-scarred years has stretched
between the Revival days of 1904-5 and these hectic, momen-
tous, fear-ridden and agnostically-minded present days of the
1960s. This book serves the worthwhile purpose of bridging
the gap between that generation and this. It brings into
true perspective the elective choice and preparation of these
servants of God together with their response to His claims.

" Pastor Dan " and " Jones," as they were and still are
affectionately known and remembered, were men of like
passions as we. Encompassed by infirmity, they became
nevertheless men of God, Apostle and Prophet, the willing
instruments of Divine purpose. The Apostolic vision center-
ing in the Headship of Christ, embracing all Spirit-baptized
members of the Church which is His body and climaxing
in the presentation to Himself of the glorified company of
the redeemed—these and the other correlated truths became
their all-absorbing passion : the stewardship committed to
them as to Paul. To declare the unsearchable riches of
Christ was their life work. For this they lived and in this
faith they died awaiting a glorious resurrection when those

won through their life and ministry will shine with them as the stars and be their joy and crown of rejoicing.

We are greatly indebted to Pastor T. N. Turnbull for his able collation and presentation of such a wealth of interesting and instructive material concerning these two servants of God. I am confident this book will have a wide circulation and an enthusiastic reception.

May the rich blessing of the Lord rest alike on writer and readers, inspiring us all with like precious faith as governed these early custodians and pioneers of the truth. "God buries His workmen but carries on His work." They have fulfilled their day and generation and now rest from their labours. Ours it is to carry the torch of revelation forward into the coming days until our Lord returns.

D. T. RENNIE,

President, General Council.

April, 1963.

CONTENTS

FOREWORD

ILLUSTRATIONS

ACKNOWLEDGEMENTS

I AM greatly indebted to the late Pastor T. Davies, Penygroes, for materials incorporated in this book. Without his painstaking preservation of details of the life and work of Pastors D. P. and W. J. Williams, this biography would have been bereft of many of the facts contained therein. I am also indebted to the writings of both Pastors D. P. and W. J. Williams, to the personal recollections of Mrs. M. T. Williams, the widow of Pastor D. P. Williams, and other members of the Williams' families.

Acknowledgement must be made to the Rev. Ionawr H. Williams, Pastor D. P. Williams's eldest son, who has allowed me freely to use memoranda about his father. I acknowledge my indebtedness to him and the others who have helped me in this way.

I am also deeply indebted to certain Pastors and members of the Apostolic Church, who have gone over the manuscript to verify the statements therein, made helpful suggestions on it, corrected the phraseology, and helped in its publication.

Finally I thank the many Pastors who spoke at the funeral services of both Pastors D. P. and W. J. Williams, and who then made statements some of which have been inserted in this book. Help has also been derived from others.

It is my desire that God will bless this joint biography to all who read it.

T. N. TURNBULL

Belfast, 1963

PART I

REVEILLE

CHAPTER ONE

THE WILLIAMS FAMILY

THE peaceful mining village of Penygroes, Carmarthenshire, stands on the brow of the Great Mountain, overlooking the rich valley of the Amman. In summer, it is surrounded by exquisite scenery. In winter, it is exposed to wind and rain.

At the end of the 19th century, Welsh was the language spoken in Penygroes. Even today, Welsh rather than English is the current speech and that most deeply appreciated.

Almost a mile to the south of the village stands ' Garnfoel,' a quaint, four-roomed cottage, nestling in a declivity of rock and crag. It was once thatched, but later was given a tiled roof, and it was here that were born the first pioneers of the present-day Apostolic Church. And it is here that the Church's headquarters are located.

In this cottage William and Esther Williams, the parents of the subjects of this biography, began their married life. Of the twelve children born to them, three died at an early age, leaving six sons and three daughters. Two of the sons were Daniel Powell Williams and William Jones Williams, with whose lives we are here specially concerned. Daniel was born on May 5, 1882, and William on May 9, 1891.

As a result of his having contracted rheumatic fever, William, the father, gradually became blind. Only 34 at the time, this was to him a bitter experience. He had a growing family to support, and the handicap was terrible.

It was pathetic too. When William Jones Williams was ten months old, his father saw him for the last time. He was the seventh child of the family.

Despite the size of the family and the father's blindness, all were well fed and clothed. Providence did not fail them. By the courage of the father, by the sacrifice and diligence of the mother, and above all by the loving kindness of God, they weathered the storms of life.

Although blind, the father achieved miracles in gardening, cobbling, basket-making, sewing and, most of all, by his skill in digging and chiselling stones which he sold for building purposes. Later, he opened a little business in the village. His efforts and skill excited wonder in those who knew him. The mother cared for her family devotedly. And before long the children contributed to the welfare and comfort of the home.

All helped in the large garden, and even after losing his sight, the father took a great interest in it and would weed as well as any of the others. During school holidays the children were occupied gathering coal from the colliery tips. All household chores had to be completed by Saturday night. Nothing must be left to be done on the Lord's Day.

All his life, it seems, the father was stern, austere and unrelenting in his discipline, ruling his family with a rod of iron. His wife, on the other hand, was affectionate, gentle, warm and human in her relations with them. She would rather suffer in silence than be involved in domestic strife. Unlike in personality though they were, the pair lived together in unbroken harmony. In later years, Pastor D. P. Williams enshrined a vivid description of their individual qualities in his poem, ' Elegy on My Father and Mother.'

Both parents communicated to their children a wealth of physical and mental qualities. Yet, for eighteen months, it was doubtful whether this second child, Daniel, would live.

Eventually, however, he began to thrive, and grew into a sturdy boy and youth.

As a young man, Daniel had a wild, passionate nature which, at times, was unruly and intractable. In common with the rest of us, but perhaps more markedly than most, he possessed a dual nature, one part being bad, the other good. Wilful and defiant, he was often chastised by his father. Often he would have been given of the birch more strokes than he actually did get had it not been for the gentle intervention of his mother. " William bach, don't whip him any more," she would plead. " Yes, I must," her husband would reply. Whereupon tears would stream down the mother's face. " I beg of you," she would cry, " give him one more warning, one more chance."

Frequently, Daniel played truant from day school. In fact, the schoolmasters at the Penygroes Council School were hard put to it to impart to him the rudiments of an education, a circumstance he was bitterly to regret in later years. Yet he did acquire English, having, as he said, " picked it up by the way," much to the astonishment of his former masters.

In his youth, Daniel had an uncontrollable temper. In later years, he said in one of his sermons, " No man could manage me as a boy. I was hysterical in fits of rage. I would tear everything up. Father and mother could not control me, and I could not control myself." The bouts of passion would not last long, however, and afterwards he would be full of remorse. Weeping he would exclaim : " What a fool I am thus to give vent to my feelings."

After his conversion he prayed : " Lord, I have a devil in me. Please will you take it out of me, and cleanse and purge me, and give me a pure soul. Lord, I beseech you to overhaul my personality, that I may be longsuffering." Later, looking back on his life, he said : " I marvel at what I am. I do not find the old demonic power dominating me, now that

Jesus has performed such a mighty work in my life. By the grace of God, it is a long time since I lost my temper."

He believed that he had inherited this passionate disposition from his grandfather, and alleged this relative in his temper "used the sledge to hit the roof of the colliery."

Nevertheless, beneath the stubborn, rebellious nature there were deep religious sensibilities, due, no doubt, to the gracious influences of his mother. Both parents were churchgoers, and this, too, had its beneficial bearing on his life. The religious atmosphere of the home, created by hymn singing, as well as the recitation of psalms and classical Welsh poetry also had a formative effect. Prayer meetings at a chapel in Penygroes and other such services, which the Williams children were obliged by their parents to attend, played an important part in his spiritual development.

Penygroes was strongly Sabbatarian. The Lord's Day was strictly observed. Everyone able to do so attended both morning and evening services and also Sunday School in the afternoon.

Daniel was to pass through many trying experiences before he came to the place of repentance and regeneration. As we have stated, he was ten years of age when his father lost his sight. This meant that the boy was compelled at that tender age to venture into the world in search of work. He found it in the coal mine and for his labours he was paid a shilling a day. Yet the Hand which blessed and multiplied the loaves and fishes blessed those meagre earnings ; and of course, as the Williams family grew, the burden of supporting it came to be shared.

In his teens young Daniel, like most people of his age group, became restless and turbulent. He had a strong craving for unrestricted freedom, a craving held in check by his love of truth and by the stern dictates of his conscience, which kept alive in him the fear that his end might be moral ruin and shame. In this vexatious situation, he often cried to God, but nothing seemed to happen. He sought to mollify his anxiety by reading hymns and psalms and by praying, but his doubts remained unresolved. Even the reading of Bunyan's ' Pilgrim's Progress ' and similar spiritual literature, had on him but a temporary influence for good.

From the feelings of frustration resulting from this tension, he found relief in competitive concerts and Eisteddfodic activities, and almost reached the topmost pinnacle as an elocutionist, becoming very popular in the recital of Welsh classical and modern poetry, and winning awards and medals. This cultivation of his voice and the platform training proved of great value in later years, his oratorical skill being used by God to enhance his power over vast congregations, who listened to him with rapt attention.

In his early years Daniel met with several accidents and endured great physical suffering. Daring and defiant, he had very little sense of danger. His escapades, often foolish, evoked the anger of his father and the anxiety of his mother.

Daniel was so fond of horses that he spent a long time one day chasing a wild horse in the fields. Having captured it, he got on its back, although there was no bridle with which to control it. The horse, maddened and frightened, charged from field to field. Reaching the river, it sprang across, pitching its rider into the water.

Another escapade was connected with a bicycle, which he somehow managed to procure. It had no tyres. In order to learn, he climbed to the top of a steep hill and began his downward career on his brakeless machine. Racing downhill, he was unable to stop the cycle, and was found lying unconscious near a wall, into which he had crashed. Fortunately he soon recovered.

On his way to work one morning he saw a wild horse grazing at the road side. A gentleman appearing on the scene, Daniel asked the favour of a ' leg up ' and the stranger obliged. The moment he had mounted it, the animal bolted. Frightened, Daniel tried to guide it, but could not, nor could he halt it when it turned into a by-road which was very steep and flanked by a high wall. The horse could not jump the wall, so it tossed Daniel over it, where he lay, badly injured. Carried home in great pain, he was laid up for several days.

Misfortune and mishap seemed to haunt him. One day, while working as a door-boy underground, the horse he was attending darted away with a number of trams. This happened so suddenly Daniel had no time to escape. He was caught and hurled underneath the trams, which, due to the human obstruction, became derailed, causing the horse to halt. His workmates found him well nigh crushed to death. Swathed in bandages, he was rushed home, in what seemed like a dying condition. To the astonishment of everyone, he got better, though only after a long convalescence.

Worse was to follow. Working with coaltrimmers in the pit one day, a large piece of coal crashed down on him, dislocating his right kneecap, and bruising both legs severely. He was taken home, where he lay for a long time in much pain. It was feared, in fact, that one leg would have to be amputated, but this was not necessary after all. Having fully recovered after a trying time on crutches, he returned to work yet again.

Not even now, however, had he learned his lesson. He had been working hard one day and was eager to reach the surface of the pit as soon as possible. Some coal trams came rushing towards him at speed. Instead of waiting for the slower, empty trams, whereby miners were taken to the pit top, he sprang forward meaning to board one of the trams. This defiance of the mining regulations might have cost him his life. The road was narrow, and he was crushed between the wagons and the side. Some loose stones gave way and derailed the trams—a contingency which, it seems, saved his life. Although stripped of all his upper clothing, amazingly his injuries were slight.

But the worst accident of all was yet to come. The day's work done, the miners were preparing to board the empty trams. Daniel was among them. Presently six of these wagons, each capable of accommodating eight men, approached at speed. Daniel made a sudden dash for the first carriage. A workman already seated on the tram moved smartly to give him room. But it was too late.

He slipped and fell beneath the carriages, and was mauled by the axles of the wheels, the axles being only some six inches above the ground. Dragged along for about twenty yards at high speed, carriage after carriage rolled over him, each full of workmen. The wagons were derailed, and the engineer on the surface feeling by the tug of the ropes that something was wrong, stopped the engine. The workmen lifted the carriages until they came upon poor Daniel, who was groaning pitifully.

His condition was fearful. His clothes were in shreds. His body was covered with blood, grease and coal dust ; his head was battered, his scalp opened ; his collar bone was fractured, his ribs broken, and his whole body battered and lacerated.

Hopes of recovery were slight. Months passed, during which Daniel refused to die, although no one dared to prophesy that he would live. However, through the mercy of God, the devotion of his mother and the skill of a conscientious physician, he made a very slow and painful return to health. To the end of his life, however, he carried scars and marks on his body as the result of that dreadful accident.

This was the last of his mad ventures. Trouble was still to come, but it was through no fault of his own. Once he and his brother were on their way to work, when there was an explosion in the pit. Daniel was thrown many yards. His clothes were set on fire and his flesh was covered with burning blisters. He cried out in his anguish. In the darkness, his brother rushed for help. Each second seeming like an age, he lay in pain and desperation until his workmates arrived. After wrapping him in linen, they carried him home, where he lay in a bath of oil for several weeks. Yet again, by the power and love of God, he was healed.

The Hand of the All-Seeing God was in all these experiences, and finally these adverse happenings brought Daniel to a sober frame of mind and caused him to think seriously of Divine matters. In his soul were born passionate yearnings and holy aspirations. While lying at the point of death Daniel had seen a vision of the Son of Man walking towards him, a vision which made him weep.

It was about this time that Daniel met the one who was to become his wife, Elizabeth Harries, of Llandeilo, sister of the late Isaac Harries, printer, of Llandeilo. They married, each resolving to help the other to live a good and useful life. But the serenity of the new home was soon disturbed. The voice of judgment echoed in Daniel's heart. Fear gripped him. Darkness invaded his whole being. He sought to assuage his distress in the solitude of the fields, but in vain. His sins pressed heavily upon him.

His young wife was alarmed by his prostration and despair. Months went by, but no relief came. Guilt lay heavily on his soul. His body weakened, his mind reeled, his fears were desperate. At last, however, hope dawned. Deliverance drew near. Light flashed into his heart like sunshine from the sky. A door of hope opened in the valley of Achor. He was ' not far from the Kingdom of God.'

William Jones Williams, Daniel's younger brother, played an admirable part in the life of the household. He was amenable and obedient and bore his share of the burdens of the household. In later years, Daniel said of him that his devotion to his parents was beyond praise. In fact, the last wage he received before leaving home he divided between his mother and his wife.

He was only twelve years old when he began to work in the colliery. Small and weak in appearance, he had an abundance of energy. In his work he was always alert and vigilant. Daniel and Jones worked together for a season, and, in order to spare his brother overstrain, Jones often undertook more than his share of the toil. This extra burden eventually left its effect on him. Climbing the steep gradients at the coal-face and standing cutting the coal for such long periods caused him to suffer from varicose veins in the legs. Though he seldom complained, the strain imposed by the malady must have been great.

The Puritanical upbringing of the family had no better effect on Jones than on Dan. Indifferent to home influences, he pommelled a pugnacious challenger until the latter cried out for mercy. Nor had Jones any compunction about pocketing the gold sovereign offered by a bystander to the winner of the match. Later, of course, he was to come under the healing and transforming influence of the Holy Spirit.

CHAPTER TWO

THE WELSH REVIVAL

THE years 1904-5 saw a notable revival in Wales. The Williams family had heard and read about the visitation of God which had taken place in 1859. Often Daniel had wondered whether he himself would see such an extraordinary visitation. At last it came, and what a wonderful awakening it was ! Without hesitation he flung wide the door of his heart to it, with the most fruitful consequences in his life.

In 1903 many of the people of Wales were spiritually dead, even some of those who had participated in the earlier revival. Religion, as a whole, was lifeless. Large numbers of people in the Principality were ungodly, living only for pleasure. Now a great spiritual change was about to take place in many of their hearts and lives.

In the summer of 1904 another revival broke out, greater in intensity and in its far-reaching consequences than even the religious awakening fifty years before.

Pastor W. T. Evans relates : " In a little mining village in the south of Wales lived a young collier lad named Evan Roberts. At the age of thirteen he gave his heart to Christ, and he began to pray that God would revive his country. Other Christians were at this time praying likewise, but Evan Roberts was the chief instrument to bring God's purpose to pass. God chose a simple youth out of a workman's cottage to be His instrument. Later the lad became a blacksmith. God had a further step for him to take, and he entered the Bible School of the Rev. Evan Phillips, Newcastle-Emlyn, to study for the ministry. While at this Bible School he was led to some Convention services. The meetings were very formal and cold, and the minister said : ' Is there not some-

one who will confess the Lord Jesus in his or her heart ?'
A young girl arose, and said : ' If no one else will say it, I
will, I love Jesus with all my heart.' The result was dynamic.
It was the commencement of the Welsh Revival. A wave of
spiritual ecstasy swept over the gathering, and many hearts
were set free. One of the great Welsh evangelists was present
and he prayed : ' Lord, bend me.' Young Evan Roberts, the
ministerial student, heard this prayer and also prayed: 'Lord,
bend me.' Immediately the Holy Spirit fell upon him. He
was shaken to the depths of his soul, and prostrated on the
ground, while God filled him with power from on high."

Back at his home, he called his young friends together and
asked them also to pray for the Holy Spirit. He gave them
four points to consider and in accordance with which to act :

(1) To put away all known sin.

(2) To put away every doubtful thing from their lives.

(3) To confess Christ as Saviour to others.

(4) To pray for the Holy Spirit, and then to obey Him.

The result was a visitation of the Holy Spirit that spread
blessing from church to church until all Wales was aflame
with the love of God.

The glory of God rested for over two years on some
localities. The descending fire burnt its way into the hearts
of men and women with sanctity and glory. Many were at
this time heard speaking with tongues and prophesying.
Others witnessed to God's healing power in their bodies, a
foretaste of what was to happen in the future. There was
no organization, no planning, no choirs and no preaching.
But there were many results. The planning was done by the
Holy Spirit. The advertizing was the simple personal testimony of revived Christians and newly converted sinners.

News of the revival spread quickly throughout Wales, the Holy Spirit being particularly active at New Quay, Loughor, Blaennerch and Ammanford. A workmate of Daniel's who lived at Ammanford told him of the revival. Daniel hastened to the town of Ammanford, where he witnessed tremendous scenes of revival. The people were confessing their sins and testifying to salvation, when Daniel turned to a friend and said : " This is all nonsense. Nobody knows that he is saved. I am getting out of here." He was, however, prevailed upon to remain, and soon came under conviction. From that moment, he became deeply contrite in heart.

The revival resulted in a moral transfiguration of the nation. Drunkards and reprobates were reclaimed, after conversion leading lives of purity and nobility. Many who had never been to church, offered a prayer or sang a hymn, were transformed into radiant Christians. At a later date some became members of the Apostolic Church.

One night a young girl, said to be the proudest in the district, came to a revival meeting. Seated in the gallery, she regarded the people with scorn. At 11 p.m., when the church was still packed and people falling to the floor calling to God for mercy, this girl also surrendered, crying to God for forgiveness. There and then she was saved, as were many others.

Members of churches achieved a new unity and harmony. Defaulters paid their debts and tradesmen had cause to thank God for His work in the hearts and souls of the people. Theatres and public houses were deserted, places of worship were full day and night. People as widely different as ministers of religion and notorious characters rejoiced in a common salvation. Even at railway stations hymns were sung and prayer meetings held.

Throughout the Principality, tens of thousands of people were saved, and the revival spread still farther afield, saving

countless others in all parts of the world. An echo of the
revival was found in the ' News Chronicle,' in January, 1951,
when the death of Evan Roberts was reported. The account
said : " Evan Roberts, leader of the great Welsh Revival of
1904-5, has died, aged 72. It was at Moriah, 47 years ago,
that the fire lit at Newcastle-Emlyn, began to glow, and
spread throughout Wales, and the five continents. Evan was
then 25. A year later, he retired, exhausted by nervous strain.
Now, after a long life of intercession in retirement, his body
is committed to the hallowed ground of the church where he
embarked on his mighty venture of faith."

The article went on to relate how, during the revival, the
Welsh press gave wide coverage to the event. London newspapers sent special correspondents to inquire about it. Men
like W. T. Stead and various church leaders went to investi-
gate it, and found that the revival was from God. The
obituary also recalled that the revival had resulted in the
closure of drink and gambling dens and the transformation
of human character.

Inevitably, perhaps, the tide ebbed. But the results remained. Many of the converts became pillars of the church
and proved ennobling influences in the life of their com-
munities. The newspaper ended its tribute to Wales's great
leader of revival with these words : " Mystics like Evan
Roberts are rare. He ended his days as he had planned,
an intercessor. A truly great man of God is being laid
to rest at Loughor tomorrow, and the whole of Wales mourns
her greatest prophet since the eighteenth century."

It was during the 1904-5 revival that the Williams family
found Christ. It is not difficult to imagine the effect of the
event on Daniel Williams. Great waves of religious emotion
swept over him. For some days he went amongst friends
and relatives confessing his sins. At times he was seen
prostrate in a kitchen or in a field. Even when at work

in the pit, his soul was in communion with God. To be holy became the master-passion of his soul, and he longed to make redress for his former selfishness and sins by way of definite service for Christ. This he set himself to do with passionate ardour.

Before the revival he had a longing to be a minister of the Gospel. Yet he knew he was unworthy. All the time he was shuttling between godliness and ungodliness. Now all was different.

Meeting a deacon of the Baptist Church, who was also fired by revival enthusiasm, Daniel suggested that united meetings be held, so that Penygroes might also become a centre of the divine blessing. This deacon arranged that revival meetings should be conducted in Calfaria, the local Baptist Chapel. This was in November, 1904, by which time the revival fire was spreading rapidly everywhere.

On Christmas Day, 1904, Daniel, along with William John Evans and David Henry Williams, his brother-in-law, went to Loughor to see Evan Roberts. On arriving, they found Moriah, the local church, packed to overflowing. The presence of God had so filled the place that what might otherwise have appeared a scene of disorder was characterised by a sublime spiritual orderliness.

In the afternoon Daniel found his way to the vestry at Pisgah, seeking God. Soon the prayer of William John Evans, " O Lord, bend Dan," was answered. The processes he had gone through had prepared him for anything and everything which God had to give him. Daniel, in real earnest, was soon occupied with God. When the Revivalist laid hands on him, Daniel's anguish returned. He streamed with perspiration. Weeping, he cried out in agony : " There is no hope for me, my sins are too great," and became unconscious of all around him. This unspeakably painful experience was followed by the sweetest tranquillity. The calmness of heaven filled his soul. The fire began to burn in his heart. Regaining consciousness, he found only a few of his friends remained, and in a darkened room. But in his heart was the light of a liberated soul. As he lay still on the floor, oblivious of all save the serenity which filled his heart, a girl bent over him and sang: "The gates of heaven are open wide; I see a sea of blood."

As she sang, there appeared to Daniel a vision of Christ on the Cross. Blood flowed from the Saviour's body, blood that bathed a sinner's head, making the flesh white as wool. The sinner, it was revealed to him, was none other than himself made white in the blood of the Lamb. Enraptured, he exclaimed: "I have seen Him; I have found Him!"

Weak physically, but vibrant in spirit, he proceeded to Moriah, the church where Evan Roberts was being used by the Almighty. Ever afterwards, Daniel claimed that this was the day of his salvation.

He reached home early in the morning to find the family awaiting his return, eager to hear what he had to say. There was confidence in his manner and conviction in his every word. "My dear boy," said his mother, "have you got Him at last?" "Yes, mother, I have got Him, praise the Lord." His mother went to her corner in the kitchen, and said: "O Daniel, I wonder have I got Jesus?" Instantly, the family began to call upon the Lord, and claimed salvation.

Daniel's father went through a period of great spiritual darkness, which lasted nine days. Often at night he was heard crying in the garden for light, and finally it broke upon his soul, and he became a loyal witness for the Lord to the end of his life. His one great weakness—strong drink—had caused his wife many tears because of his condition and its effects. Now drunkenness became a thing of the past, and the father raised up a family altar in the home. His wife, too, was converted at an all-night prayer meeting.

Afterwards the sons and daughters also received God's mercy. The divine visitation brought to the home the wealth of untold riches in Christ Jesus, and the cottage became in the fullest sense the Lord's sanctuary, where He was worshipped ceaselessly.

At the early age of 14, William Jones Williams decided for Christ. His voice was often heard in earnest prayer amongst the people, and on one occasion in the front seats of the gallery of a chapel at Penygroes he was heard to pray : " O Lord, grant that the taps of every cellar may become rusty, and every tap-room idle and empty, so that there shall be no more drunkards in the land."

He travelled to surrounding villages visiting revival meetings. On one occasion Evan Roberts and Dr. D. M. Phillips, M.A., Ph.D.—the latter one of the historians of the Welsh Revival—were holding a meeting in the Methodist Church at Llanllian, near Penygroes. The place was so crowded that many could not find a seat. Jones found his way up the pulpit steps and eventually found himself sitting between the two great men.

While the congregation was singing and praying, Evan Roberts said to Jones : " Do you love Jesus ?" He replied, " Of course, I love Jesus." Then Evan Roberts asked : " Would you like to become a minister ?" Jones answered : " Yes, I would indeed like to be a minister, sir." Mr. Roberts called the attention of Dr. Phillips, and said : " This boy would like to be a minister for God." And both laid their hands on him and asked God to make him a preacher of the Gospel.

Thereafter, along with other enthusiastic witnesses for Christ, Daniel began to conduct prayer meetings in the mine where he worked and through these many gave their souls to God. Among those thus reached was John Thomas, who became Sunday School Superintendent at Penygroes Apostolic Church.

Pastors D. P. and W. J. Williams
in the early years of their ministry

Garnfoel House where Pastors D. P. and W. J. Williams
were born

Apostolic Church Bible College, Penygroes,
as it was in 1935

Another was Ostler R. Morgan, of Bankrock, whose gifts as a vocalist were much in demand in the services and elsewhere.

The whole neighbourhood was now under the spell of revival and the converts were waxing strong in the Lord. Among those in the forefront was Daniel. He could not be deterred by anyone or anything. With diligence he applied himself to soul winning.

The Welsh Revival was the opening phase of a period of Pentecostal and Apostolic expansion perhaps unparalleled since the first century. Throughout the revival there came to light important truths which, hitherto, had been overlooked by the churches. Among them were the assurance of salvation, and the baptism of the Holy Spirit, as well as the need of a separated life. Also raised up out of it to reveal again the true significance of the Pauline order of Church Government were Daniel Powell Williams and William Jones Williams.

" If you fail Me now," said the Holy Spirit through Pastor W. J. Williams to Pastor D. P. Williams at the beginning of the Apostolic Church work in Penygroes, " this generation will pass away, and you shall not be an instrument in My hand to reveal My purpose of bringing again into being the scriptural order of Church Government." Pastor D. P. Williams was not disobedient to the heavenly Vision.

CHAPTER THREE

PENTECOSTAL OUTPOURING

SERMON-TASTING is a feature and perhaps a fault in religious Wales. Daniel was often to be seen following pulpit notabilities of his day. It was, in fact, under the influence of preaching, coupled with his religious bent, that he became passionately anxious to become a preacher and to enter into the ministry of the Gospel.

Convinced there was no other calling for him, he prayed earnestly and worked arduously, studying the Word of God with diligence. Also he read biographies of men who had been used to stir Wales by their preaching and piety. This acted as an immense stimulus to his aspirations.

One Friday afternoon, some two years after the Welsh Revival, he was working in the mine when the hand of God came upon him so heavily he could not continue working. With it came a distinct voice. Clear and irresistible, in origin it was obviously divine. He was to make the great surrender and to follow his Master.

Immediately, he thought of his wife and two children and of his employment. On the one hand, there were his domestic responsibilities ; on the other, a clear command from heaven. It was the supreme and crucial test of his sincerity, not to be decided lightly or hastily.

The test, though severe, was triumphantly passed. His answer was that of all the saints and servants of the Lord : " Not my will, but Thine be done." He also prayed to God, if this were His will, he would be approached on the matter within a fortnight's time by the minister and deacons of the chapel he attended.

Before the fortnight ended, the minister broached to Daniel the matter of his becoming a minister. Was Daniel willing to answer the call to preach the Gospel as a local preacher with the congregational cause ? If so, the minister promised to bring the matter before the church.

It was clear that Daniel was destined to play a leading part in the purposes of God. But still he had his doubts, having had neither a secondary education, nor a theological training. He had no library of any worth, nor had he sermonic talent. But two deacons approached him and assured him that they were convinced of his call to the ministry.

At this juncture a Methodist minister, the Rev. Ffinant Morgan, B.A., B.D., took him one Sunday to Loughor where he himself was to preach. In the evening, he asked Daniel to read the lesson and to lead in prayer. For the first time Daniel opened a service. This was the same church in which he had known the experience which so transformed his life.

Returning home, he assured his minister and deacons that he would respond to the call. When the matter was placed before the church, the congregation stood up, without exception, to signify their approval of his call. For his trial sermon, he took as text : " Upon this rock I will build my Church, and the gates of Hell shall not prevail against it." The trial sermon was found satisfactory and was much appreciated. No doubt it was prophetic of the ministry that followed.

On the following Sunday night he divided his efforts between two small country chapels. Having put his hand to the plough, he never once looked back, and was to lead many souls to Christ. In addition, he was unsparing in his private meditation and in reading and studying the scriptures, his aim being to make himself an effective minister. All this time he was engaged in his work as a miner, for he earned too little as a preacher to give up his manual toil.

For almost six years he covered an extensive area as a local preacher, ministering during the period in almost 80 chapels. The frequent calls for his ministry at special services and missions made it imperative that he should relinquish work in the pit in order to devote his whole time to the Master's service. Later, he was offered the pastorate of two Congregational churches, but felt led to decline both. He was a preacher of considerable power. The Rev. Towyn Jones, minister of New Bethel, Glanamman, who later became an M.P. and a Liberal Whip, said to him after hearing him preach : " Go on, my boy, I believe a great work awaits you. Don't be afraid to preach that sermon throughout the country. You preach like a coming prophet."

Yet he had many discouragements. On one occasion, his uncle, the Rev. J. J. Williams, sent for Daniel to preach at his church at Llangybi, Cardiganshire. After working in the mine on Saturday morning from 3 a.m. until 8 a.m., he walked up to the top of the mine. Weary and thirsty, he reached the surface. After a wash and some breakfast, he set out for the village of Dryslwyn, some seven miles away, was caught in the rain, and then had the mortification of missing his train. He pressed on, but was so overcome with fatigue that he was tempted to send a telegram to inform his uncle of his decision to return home. Nevertheless he went on, walking most of the way, and preached the following day, afterwards walking home to Penygroes. As an outcome of this experience he had a breakdown in health and was ill for three months. A gentleman from Aberaeron was led by God to take him away for five weeks' holiday. Afterwards Daniel was able to resume his employment.

In straitened circumstances, his job and health gone, still his faith did not waver. Referring later to this period of his life, he said : " We may prove God and have rapturous experiences in our moral and spiritual services for the Lord, but when His movements begin to touch the material and physical, and to affect our temporal welfare, something vital in our nature is touched, and unless the supernatural is invoked to help us through, nothing else will."

At this time, the high tide of spiritual fervency was waning, but in certain areas of Wales new Mission Halls were keeping the revival burning. The emphasis during the revival was on the ' New Birth ' and the ' Assurance of Salvation,' with a measure of God's baptismal fulness. In 1907-8 there was experienced in England, Scotland and Wales a mighty outpouring of the Holy Spirit with signs following, and a manifestation of the nine gifts of the Holy Spirit. This second visitation of God appeared like a further revelation of truth. The ground for this visitation had been well prepared at Penygroes, so that many Christians received the baptism of the Holy Spirit. Many families experienced this, including that of the Williams's at " Garnfoel " cottage. Almost all its members had the baptism of the Holy Spirit with signs following.

Belle Vue, Swansea, became a centre of unforgettable blessings. Rapturous were the manifestations embodying all that was sublime and holy. At first, Daniel remained a cautious onlooker, resolved to be sure that these things were of God before he gave them his approval. Pastor W. Phillip records as follows what happened when Daniel received the baptism of the Holy Spirit.

" In 1909, nearly five years after Daniel's conversion, he went to Aberaeron for a holiday and there met a company of God's people who were baptized with the Holy Spirit. Daniel joined them and climbed a hill overlooking the bay. Here, as they were praising God, Daniel fell flat on his face, weeping, sobbing, and groaning, and he received the mighty baptism of the Holy Spirit. Ecstasy overwhelmed his soul, and he spoke with tongues as the Holy Spirit gave him utterance. As sure as Pentecost began a new era for the world, so this Pentecost began a new era in the life of this lay preacher. He had studied for the ministry, but he still required the power of the Holy Spirit. Now he had received that power."

Later, on coming down the hill, they saw a crowd of people being entertained by a clown. Daniel, full of the Holy Spirit, began to exhort the people to lift their hearts to something higher. The clown, annoyed, marshalled the crowd against Daniel and a fight broke out. But a friend saved the day. The fight was halted and Daniel went on with his sermon. No small stir was created when the clown washed the paint from his face and sang with the company.

Daniel continued to preach in the churches, but also held services with those who believed in the baptism of the Holy Spirit. Specially arranged meetings were held, and during these God's Spirit manifested His presence in a mighty way by the gifts of the Holy Spirit. These manifestations were gradually being understood and their benefits appreciated. The company of believers who had received the baptism of the Holy Spirit had grown greatly. Eventually, they built the Evangelistic Hall at Penygroes.

Now, Daniel had to make a decision whether to detach himself from the Welsh Congregationalists and join the new company wholeheartedly or remain poised between the two. The thought of severing his connections with a circle which had helped him towards distinction was intensely disagreeable to him. He had ministerial appointments covering the next twelve months, and these would have to be cancelled. His indecision became so burdensome that it was almost more than he could endure. In the end, he knew that separation had to come. He tendered his resignation and cancelled his engagements.

Eventually, he heard the voice of God through a Prophet,

giving a personal message to himself, and it was so un-
mistakable, searching and profound that he fell on his face
in deep contrition and brokenness of heart. He learnt that
he had been chosen by God for a work hitherto not revealed
to him. Also another word that came to him was : " On the
morrow thou shalt be buried in baptism with thy Lord," and
this did indeed take place on the following day.

Later, when two servants of the Lord visited Penygroes,
the brethren of the Evangelistic Hall bade them welcome.
During the visit they called at the home of Daniel's elder
brother, the cottage in which his mother had been born.
Whilst the ministers were praying for a sick child of the
household, the Holy Spirit descended on the mother and
baptized her. This was simply a preliminary blessing to
prepare Daniel for a further revelation of God's will. One
of the brethren began to prophesy, and indicated that the
moment of revelation had come. God was about to make
known His choice concerning the shepherd of the flock.
Daniel was revealed as God's choice for this position. Hands
were laid on him, making him the Shepherd of Penygroes
assembly. Then one of the visitors told him that the word
had been given them before they came to Penygroes to the
effect that they should anoint the Lord's servant in a farm
in the presence of a company of people whom the Lord
would bring together without any previous arrangement.
The company had gathered together as foretold. Daniel's
ordination was carried out and the day was spent in prayer.

On this Daniel later commented : " The Cross was working
with caustic effect, but at the same time I knew that God's
movements were beyond question." It was about this time
that Daniel Williams received the Apostolic Vision, and ever
afterwards was inspired and dominated by it. He lived for
it, toiled for it and eventually died for it. The voice of

God was heard in the midst through certain channels, and it was confirmed that the one ordained was to take charge.

From that hour he took up the leadership and set his face towards the goal of complete obedience to his Lord. He had an unswerving faith, an unflinching courage and an indomitable resolve. It was in 1911 that he finally left his employment as a miner and became a full-time minister.

After the fervour of the Welsh Revival had abated, Jones became for a time spiritually cold. He and one of his sisters were the only two in the family who did not go on with the Lord. For six years he was a backslider. Naturally speaking, he had an industrious nature, and was prosperous in all he undertook.

In that spiritual state Jones found it difficult living in a home where all were regenerated. He worked with Daniel in the pit, and Dan used every means to bring the prodigal back to Christ, but without effect. A good-living young man, he was a member of the Congregational Chapel at Penygroes and a regular communicant, yet he was a rebel against God's mercy and love. Once, he went to hear a missionary speak at the Evangelistic Hall and conviction rested so strongly upon him he jumped over four seats in order to get away from the challenge of the spiritual environment.

At that time his unsaved sister became seriously ill, and the missionary went to visit her. It was after midnight when Jones reached home that night, as he had no wish to meet the missionary. Nearing the house, he heard an active repetition of the scene described in Luke 15—music and dancing. Entering, he saw his sister dancing with spiritual joy. When she opened her eyes and saw him, she ran to him, threw her arms around his neck and cried : " Jones, Jesus has saved me and healed me !"

Having, in his condition of mind and heart, no one else as companion, he arranged with his mother for a friend of his to come and lodge with him. Jones was the sole support of the family at that time, so his mother gave her consent, although she was not happy about it. The young man was a pugilist and very worldly, but the influence of the godly home soon had its effect on him. One Sunday, when Jones was away from home, the young man went to the Evangelistic Hall and was converted. When Jones returned to the cottage that night, and learned what had happened, he felt that he was utterly alone.

During the first fortnight following the salvation of this pugilist, there were fourteen converts in Daniel's assembly. The Holy Spirit descended and the fourteen converts were baptized with the Holy Spirit. The same night some Christians in the Evangelistic Hall were holding a prayer meeting, and God visited them and baptized them with the Holy Spirit. At the same moment a few Christians had called at the home of a deacon of the chapel, and they, too, received the same experience. As a result of all these happenings the Apostolic Church made a modest beginning in Penygroes, and thus was born a movement which has spread throughout the world.

The time came when God revealed His purpose for Jones. A special unction was on the gathering one night when God spoke to Pastor D. P. Williams through his former friend, Ivor Thomas, in English, the date being February, 1911 :

" Hearken thou unto My word, My servant. I have a purpose for thee this night, to go on My word to the home of thy brother (Ivor). Thou shalt find two young men there. Deliver unto them this message : ' My Spirit shall not always strive with man.' For I have a great purpose for one of them, that he shall stand at thy side in the days that are coming, and he shall travel with thee to many lands, for he is a chosen vessel unto Me. Yea, a channel shall he be in Mine hand, saith the Lord. Prove thou Me, my servant, and fear not, for it shall come to pass, saith the Lord."

Pastor D. P. Williams obeyed. In his brother's home he found two young men. The message was given, and prayer was offered. Both followed to the Evangelistic Hall, and ultimately surrendered to Christ, one being Daniel's brother, Jones. The Lord's word literally did come to pass, for Jones, later known widely as Pastor W. J. Williams, was from that hour engaged in the Lord's work. As a Prophet he visited many lands with his brother.

The ministry of the spoken word was given progressively, and in time many profound messages were given, especially after Jones had received his baptism in the Holy Spirit and begun to prophesy. So significant were the manifestations of the Holy Spirit through him as a channel of blessing, that many were persuaded there was a specific and elective purpose for him. As we now know, the outcome of the spoken word through him has been of great value to the Apostolic Church in many nations.

PART II

ENLISTMENT

CHAPTER FOUR

APOSTOLIC BEGINNINGS

TO begin with, the small community had held cottage meetings, but afterwards thay had gathered in local rooms in Penygroes. In 1910 the Evangelistic Hall was built. In time misunderstanding and prejudice caused division in the midst. To avoid further controversy, it was decided that those who accepted the Apostolic Church vision and revelation should withdraw and establish a place of their own. This happened in 1911.

From the outset, the Church established in Penygroes was known as the Apostolic Church. The members met in different buildings from time to time, first in the vestry of a Congregational Chapel (Soar), then in a butcher's shop, and later in a salt store. Afterwards for nine months the services were carried on in the Council School. Eventually the leaders and members were directed by the prophetic word to secure a sectional building, and this was kept in the garden of the home of David John Jones. Later a piece of land was bought and the sectional building, known as the ' Babell,' was erected. Built on a brick foundation, it was covered with corrugated iron sheets. The word ' Babell ' means ' Tabernacle ' or ' Tent of Meeting.' Gatherings were held there until 1933, when the congregation moved some one hundred yards or so south of the newly-erected Apostolic Temple.

The Church properties acquired were placed under proper legal trusteeship by Pastor D. P. Williams, the firm of solicitors chosen being Messrs. Gee and Edwards. Later, in the year 1916, the Tenets of the Apostolic Church were approved by Pastor D. P. Williams and his associates, as that was necessary in order that they should be inserted in the Trust Deed concerning Church lands and buildings.

Daniel now had a message to proclaim, and this became the great business of his life. Previously, he had been a very popular preacher in the Congregational Church. Now he no longer sought popularity. Rather he desired to proclaim the Apostolic message, which included the five ascension gifts of Christ, and the nine gifts of the Holy Spirit, a message which he did not expect to be accorded a favourable reception. In his heart there was a vision, and he was consumed with a burning zeal to make it known to the people.

He realized, too, that there would devolve on him heavy pastoral duties. The newly launched barque was beset by many storms, but with God's help he piloted it through the troubled waters.

In those early years there was for the pastor no promise of a stated salary. This was an initial test of his faith. On one occasion, at the end of a month, he had nothing to give to his wife for the support of a growing family. That night a man came to the house and thrust a few shillings into his hand. Little did that benefactor know that Daniel had spent the day fasting and praying for a sign of the Divine approval in matters touching the needs of the home.

Later, a freewill offering box was placed in the sanctuary that those who believed in his calling might show their goodwill. Time after time the hand of the Lord provided, changing despair into joy. Again and again the Pastor tightened his belt, and always, whatever his circumstances, he faithfully pursued the course laid down for him.

In the new building charismatic phenomena were in evidence. The bliss was such that it seemed as if the people had already entered into heaven. The Spirit of the Lord was manifested mightily. The nine gifts of the Holy Spirit were in operation continually, especially the voice gifts, divers kinds of tongues, interpretation of tongues, and prophecy. There was likewise healing and restoration of spirit, soul and body. By signs and wonders the Lord proved the veracity of His word.

Conspicuous as a case of healing was that of the saintly Mr. Thomas, of Glanglesnant. His doctor had told him he would soon die. A sister-in-law of the sick man was in the house when Daniel and some of the brethren visited him. She said to Daniel, " You must not be too long in the bedroom, Thomas is not well, and you might disturb him." They stood around the bed and prayed for the invalid. At the same time Mr. Thomas was praying, " Lord, if you are going to heal me, tell Mr. Williams to lay his hand on my head and command me to be made whole."

Daniel did not know of the request, but he did just as Mr. Thomas had prayed he should. " Lord," he prayed, "bless him and raise him up now." Immediately Mr. Thomas jumped out of bed and called for his clothes. He was healed. But his sister-in-law said : " You have killed Thomas. You have raised him up into some ecstasy, but that will fade and he will die." Yet, although according to medical testimony, one of Thomas's lungs was gone, he was healed so effectively that he lived for many years afterwards, a marvel to all who knew him.

Pastor D. P. Williams also visited a coloured man named Berry, who had sustained such severe injuries in an accident that the doctors marvelled that he was alive. He had recovered to the extent of moving about, but he fell easily and was unable to rise without help. He could only walk by bending heavily upon a stick. He received the baptism of the Holy Spirit, but was physically no better.

Attending a meeting being held by Daniel, he came to the platform at the close of the service seeking Divine healing. He was anointed with oil, and the moment hands were laid on him he jumped and leaped. Then he took off his coat and boots and put them on again, which he had been unable to do since his accident.

The next week Daniel and Mr. Berry were in a motor-car that developed a puncture. At Daniel's request, Mr. Berry, a big man, lifted the car in order that the jack might be placed under the wheel. This was ample evidence that the healing had been complete and permanent.

Soon there was opposition to the movement in the daily and weekly newspapers and in religious periodicals. Yet Daniel persisted on the high course he was set to pursue, and continued to preach and practise the scriptural truths revealed to him. This provoked criticism and warnings from pulpit and platform, and also attacks in newspapers and religious journals.

In this atmosphere of hostility a Movement was brought to birth that has become universal in its blessing and limitless in its possibilities. It is a glowing tribute to the integrity and loyalty of certain brethren, including Pastors D. P. and W. J. Williams that, during the infant stages of the work, in spite of much opposition and persecution they continued with unswerving fidelity to promote the vision vouchsafed to them.

The greatest revelation of that time was that God's Prophet had come to sight, one who would accompany his brother, the Apostle, on his world-wide travels, and that the prophetic word might be heard wherever and whenever there was a willing listener.

The fact that the Word of the Lord was being declared in the ' Babell ' was so noised abroad there was no need to make announcements. Believers and unbelievers came there from the surrounding villages and districts. God began to work among companies in these places, and the leaders from the Apostolic Church in Penygroes made visits to such gatherings. Later, a special Convention was held in Belle Vue Church, Swansea. Daniel was invited to speak at the gathering, but as he had ministered only in Welsh until now, and would on this occasion have had to speak in English, he was reluctant to accept the invitation. Divine guidance through prophetical ministry directed him to go to the Convention and to take with him his brother, Jones. The special services brought new revelation of God's purpose to many, and also brought Daniel into touch with many other assemblies God had visited with the Pentecostal outpouring.

In Pastor W. Jones Williams the prophetic gift matured, and it often happened that the company were kept before the Lord until the late hours of the night, listening to the mighty utterances that poured through him. The Prophet W. J. Williams was young and had never been privileged to study the works of the theologians nor those of the authorities on the doctrines of Scripture. In fact, his knowledge of the Bible was very limited. But men of advanced knowledge and well versed in Scripture listened in amazement while the Spirit of God unfolded through him the depths of divine truth. Another proof of the divinity of the prophetic word was the correct language used, as though Jones were an educated man, when, in fact, he was not. All who knew him were constrained to acknowledge that none other than God the Holy Spirit spoke through him. In those early days many waxed strong in the faith, and were confirmed and established as they believed the prophets.

The prophetic word at this time was used to call Brother Roderick as a missionary attached to the Apostolic Faith Church. He was located at Johannesburg for a time. Others who were chosen were David Jones, of Bryntirion, Daniel

Williams, Evan Thomas, Evan Jenkins, Cwmcoch, and W. J. Evans, all of whom became elders at Penygroes to help Pastor D. P. Williams. They were the first to be ordained by him, and it brought joy to his heart. Later William Howells was called as an elder. Rees Evans was for a time Overseer at the 'Babell.' Later still David Jones, Bryn Road, and Rufus Davies were called as elders.

Many who had been converted were in debt to the tradesmen of Penygroes village. The Holy Spirit warned them that they were to owe no man anything and that no open-air services were to be held until the debts were paid. They were commanded by the Holy Spirit to collect money to pay these debts. By the end of twelve months £150 had been gathered and all debts were liquidated. "Now are ye free to go and preach and testify," came the prophetic word.

Presently, contacts were made with the Apostolic Faith Church in Bournemouth, and for a number of years the Welsh assemblies were joined to that fellowship. In 1915, however, Pastor D. P. Williams, and most of the presbyteries of the many Welsh assemblies deemed it wise to withdraw from it. Events proved that the Welsh brethren had been guided rightly in their decision.

Pastor D. P. Williams was called to the Apostleship in a Convention in London, in 1913, while still connected with the Church in Bournemouth. A humble man, he found it hard to believe he was an Apostle. He sobbed and groaned and wished to run away from this great call of God. He went home wondering what the elders at Penygroes would say, but everyone embraced him, and all the officers in the other assemblies acknowledged his call.

Jones was also called into the full-time ministry. The work had so greatly increased that the presbyteries of the assemblies decided to give him this call. Demands from all directions were made on the two brothers, allowing them hardly time

Pastors D. P. and W. J. Williams, and other Pastors
from Wales and Glasgow on their first visit to
Glasgow and Belfast in January, 1920

Pastors D. P. and W. J. Williams and Pastor A. Turnbull in
Nigeria in 1931

Apostolic Temple, Penygroes

Apostolic Church, Copenhagen,
visited by Pastors D. P. and W. J. Williams in 1924
and later years

to rest. Jones afterwards claimed that he was ordained to the ministry three times, before the foundation of the world, during the Welsh Revival when Evan Roberts laid hands on him, and also in the Apostolic Church. Thus the Lord's choice was revealed, that the gift of apostle was to have the gift of the prophet at his side, as in the Early Church.

The work continued to increase, and many people visited Penygroes, some coming from distant places. The correspondence of Pastor D. P. Williams increased greatly, so that an Apostolic Church Office had to be established in a room at Clifton House, Llwynhendy, near Llanelly, the home of Pastor T. Jones, the first Apostle called after Pastor D. P. Williams. Pastor T. Jones administered the financial statements and literature, with the help of his son Omri, and the Scribe T. Davies acted as shorthand writer and typist. Accounts and circulars were issued from this office. It was now arranged that the office work should be centred in Penygroes, with the Scribe T. Davies doing the clerical work and Pastor D. C. Morgan acting as Treasurer.

The office, built of timber, was to be erected on ground adjacent to the house of Pastor D. P. Williams. Prophetical ministry through Pastor W. J. Williams revealed that by the time the building was ready, the money would be available. As a token of this, the Lord said : " Tomorrow thou shalt receive ten pounds as a sign that this is My will." To their dismay, nothing came by the morning's mail. But, at midday, a telegraphic order came for £10. Before the building was completed it was, in fact, paid for, as the Holy Spirit had declared.

The first number of the " Riches of Grace," the official magazine of the Apostolic Church, was issued in April, 1916. For many years Pastor D. P. Williams was its editor, and the circulation of the magazine has spread all over the world.

Then, as now, the nearest railway station to Penygroes

was four miles away. To overcome the transport difficulty, prayer was made for the provision of a motor car. The prophetic reply came : " A swift chariot I will send you soon, so that you may be able to travel according to the demands of My will, and I would have you to prepare a garage." The garage was built and, as soon at it was completed, a new Ford car was donated to the assembly. This proved of great value, being used at all hours and generally being filled with God's servants travelling in response to the increasing and varied calls.

Passing through a village one day, the brethren stopped the car and held an open-air meeting, the car serving as pulpit. At the end of the service prophetical ministry declared : " I will gather in this place a people unto Myself." Today, there is an Apostolic Church in that place, with a company of faithful members.

On the many journeys made in the car, several accidents or narrow escapes took place. On one occasion a broken axle might have resulted in serious injury. The car went careering down the steep road from Hirwaun to Glynneath. The occupants called upon the Lord. The speed of the car was materially reduced by a rise in the roadway, thus allowing the driver to turn it into the ditch without mishap.

One day whilst driving along they were appalled to see a child standing right in the track of the car. Pastor W. J. Williams swung the vehicle towards a steep bank. It cleared it and came to rest in the field beyond. When a crowd gathered to express their resentment, he explained what had happened, and it dawned on them that the driver had risked his life to save that of the child.

There was, however, what might have been a catastrophe in America in 1922, when Pastors D. P. and W. J. Williams, Andrew Turnbull and Frank Hodges were returning to Philadelphia after a 3,000 mile journey visiting churches in U.S.A. and Canada. They were on a by-road, with the sun shining strongly on the windscreen of the car, when the driver came suddenly to a sharp turn in the road. As the car spun round its full weight was forced on to the back right wheel, the wooden spokes splintering to pieces. The car somersaulted twice into a field and finished with the four men underneath it. Pastors D. P. Williams and A. Turnbull were the most seriously injured, but the temporary physical shaking soon became negligible under the healing hand of God. All four experienced a miraculous escape.

On May 23, 1918, Pastor D. P. Williams suffered the loss of his wife, Elizabeth. She had upheld him in times of stress, and in the problems of his early years as preacher and minister. She had borne him seven children, Eirian, Ionawr, Omri, Bronwen, Moelwyn, Picton and Florence, and she had been a true mother to them all.

After an interval, Pastor D. P. Williams married Miss Mabel Thomas, of Porthcawl. She was certainly needed to care for the young family. Mabel's systematic, Puritan training served her in good stead and she was to the seven children a wise and understanding mother. In the years that followed she was used by God to minister in Women's Meetings and by writing articles for the " Riches of Grace."

Pastor D. P. Williams's deep compassion for others in bereavement was born of his own experiences. Not only did he lose his first wife, Elizabeth, but also a baby girl, Esther Maria, and his daughter, Olwen, when she was only seven years old. In 1924, the Lord took his son Moelwyn, aged thirteen years. The Pastor was comforted that each of them had gone to be with Christ, which is far better.

Some years previously, on May 11, 1917, his father had passed away to be with the Lord. He was 59 years of age. On May 8, 1923, his mother also went to her heavenly home. She was 63 years of age. At the end she said to Daniel and

Jones : " My dear boys, I am quite ready and content to go home, and I am leaving you behind to serve Jesus." For the last eighteen years of her life she had lived joyously and triumphantly as a Christian.

Pastors D. P. and W. J. Williams often spoke of the visit of two angels to their home, just before the death of their father. Jones was sitting at his father's bedside when he heard steps approaching the house. The blind father heard the steps also. At the time, Jones went down to the parlour for some ice to quench his father's thirst. He was passing through the kitchen when he heard a knock on the door. Two men came into the house and sat down. Their faces were shining and they looked straight towards the window. Jones knew they were angels, and he was rather dazed and frightened when passing them. He dared not ask them any questions, and they remained in the house until the dawn.

When Pastor D. P. Williams prayed for an explanation, prophetical ministry came through his brother saying : " If Jones had had the courage to speak to the angels, they would have stated that one angel had come to take the father home in a few days, and the other angel had come to take a young child in the family soon afterwards." At the time the word was given none of the children of either Pastor was ill. Soon afterwards, however, the young daughter of Pastor W. J. Williams was taken to be with Christ. Many a time afterwards Christians came to ' Garnfoel ' to sit in the chairs where the angels sat.

Of the brothers and sisters of Pastors D. P. and W. J. Williams, Mr. David John Williams died on December 13, 1949, aged 69 years, a faithful elder of the Apostolic Church at Penygroes, and latterly of Pontlliw. Mr. Ivor Williams, a faithful elder of the Apostolic Church at Ammanford, died in March, 1962. Surviving members of the family at the time of writing are : Mrs. James Swithenbank, Mrs. Ivor

Thomas, a member of the Apostolic Church, Penygroes, Mrs. D. H. Williams also of the same Church, Mr. Stephen Williams, a deacon of Crosshands Apostolic Church, and Mr. Drummond Williams, Penygroes.

The flame of revival burned in the hearts of the children, and the faithfulness of Daniel and Jones brought spiritual blessing to the family of William and Esther Williams, of ' Garnfoel.' Mother and father await a blessed resurrection, their bodies being interred in the graveyard of the Welsh Congregational Chapel, ' the Square,' Penygroes. Out of their family have sprung three generations, many of them carrying with them a saving knowledge of the gracious Redeemer and a compelling testimony of His goodness and grace.

PART III

INTO BATTLE

CHAPTER FIVE

ON THE HOME FRONT

THE work thus initiated by God was by this time rapidly developing. The two brothers, Pastors D. P. and W. J. Williams, were being used of God as Apostle and Prophet by acts and deeds under the power of the Holy Spirit. Their earliest efforts had been more or less confined to Penygroes and district. Now they moved out to wider fields in Wales and elsewhere in Britain.

In 1913, when they were forty miles from home, the two Pastors and a fellow Christian went up a mountain which gave them a broad view of valleys in which lived many thousands of people. There Pastor D. P. Williams prayed, asking that they might possess the towns they could see, inheriting them in God's name. The Holy Spirit replied, through Pastor W. J. Williams, that the prayer would be answered.

Thereafter they travelled far and near, night and day, in sunshine and storm, in Wales and other countries, and they did possess villages, towns and cities as God had promised. In one place the people said of them : " We do not understand these Apostolic Pastors. When they visit a place, they always leave an Apostolic Church behind them."

In nearby towns assemblies were established and set in order, elders and deacons being appointed. Soon Pastor Thomas Jones was called to the full-time ministry and proved to be a most devout and faithful Pastor, and later, a most worthy Apostle.

As a Prophet, Pastor W. J. Williams played an important part at Pastor T. Jones's side for a season. In due time Pastor T. Jones's son, Omri, was called as a Prophet and he became one of the most valuable Prophets in the Church. Indeed, his services in that capacity cannot be over-estimated.

With a view to opening new assemblies many series of Special Meetings were held in Wales. These sometimes met with instant success. At other times they excited great opposition.

Such services were conducted in Aberaeron and Llanon. The Cardiganshire people, famed as being hard-headed and somewhat cautiously conservative, were not kindly disposed towards the movement at first. Pastors D. P. and W. J. Williams, along with Mr. Stephen Bowen, visited Llanon to establish an assembly. In one meeting prophetical ministry commanded Pastor J. J. Williams to read from Acts 17. After he had read the following verses : " But the Jews which believed not, moved with envy, took unto them certain lewd fellows of the baser sort, and gathered a company, and set all the city in an uproar, and assaulted the house of Jason and sought to bring them out to the people." Later prophetical ministry indicated that the Pastors in Llanon would experience within a short time a disturbance similar to that in the Early Church.

Soon this word was fulfilled. At one meeting they were interrupted by a shower of stones, windows being broken. Pastor D. P. Williams had been warned by the police that the little company was in some danger. Daniel replied that he must preach the Gospel no matter what the consequences might be. A serious situation developed, and some of the brethren were shamefully treated. One opposer was badly hurt when a splinter of stone pierced his arm. It came from a window-sill he had blown to pieces with dynamite.

The outcome was police court proceedings. The 'Welsh Gazette' said of the case : " No blame was attached to the Apostolic Pastors, but they were brought into the case that justice might be done. They made it clear to the police and the villagers that they bore no grudge whatever for the treatment meted out to them."

At the time of the riots and violence, the Vicar of Llanon told his parishioners : " If this is not of God it will soon wither away." He was right. But as the Apostolic Church is of God, it has greatly prospered in all the five continents. Pastor W. J. Williams's life, in danger at Llanon, was again in danger from opponents of the truth at Aignon, in France, and also in Australia, the Lord preserving him in all these perils.

The work accomplished by Pastor D. P. Williams was truly astonishing, as his diary testifies. In 1920, he was at the Swansea Assembly on March 7. On the 8th, he was at home working, until he went to Swansea in the evening. On the 13th he was at Skewen, on the 14th at Penygroes, and on the 15th at Ystalyfera, each week being crowded with meetings and travelling, with services and preparations for services, and other church administration work, in addition to visiting the members of the church.

In the years 1916-1919 the work greatly prospered in Wales. As it did so, the activities of Pastor D. P. Williams also increased. It is, indeed, testimony to the sustaining grace of the Holy Spirit that Pastor Williams was able to accomplish so much. Physically weak because of what had happened to him during his years in the mines, the Lord strengthened him, and his physical weakness in no way hindered the work. He was a perpetual miracle, and all who knew him marvelled at his accomplishments.

Having read the history of Evan Roberts and of the Welsh Revival, he prayed with his wife for a spiritual revival, asking that he, himself, might be used to establish the Church anew. The years 1919-1924 marked a period of still greater progress in South Wales, many new church buildings being erected, worthy places for the public worship of God. Here is an example of how one was built.

About this time, an Apostolic elder, Thomas Richards, was visiting Crosshands, and was told by God that a place of worship would be built on a certain site in that village. At a later period, a company of baptized believers assembled in a house in Crosshands, Pastor D. C. Morgan being the Overseer. Prophetical ministry told them to buy a piece of land and build a place of worship on it. This was done, the building, seating 120, being called 'Rehoboth,' and it stands on the very site revealed to Thomas Richards. In the years ahead many more buildings were erected. This was in fulfilment of a prophetic word that came through Pastor W. J. Williams.

In the buying of land and the erection of buildings the Welsh presbyteries were helped by those members of the Church who had prospered under God's hand. These loaned money to the Church. The loans soon amounted to an appreciable figure, but the interest due was paid promptly, and the capital, too, was eventually repaid.

The work of saving souls, healing bodies, baptizing with water and the Holy Spirit went on apace. Pastor D. P. Williams and his brother visited many of the valleys in Wales, answering the calls of Christians who desired to know more of the Apostolic vision and order. These assemblies eventually joined the Apostolic Church after examining its beliefs and practices. At first, many of these assemblies laboured under much difficulty, great accusations being made against the Apostolic Church. In time, however, the hindrances vanished and the work of the Holy Spirit proceeded.

Their visits to so many places resulted in hundreds of souls being converted. It was wonderful to see drunkards, gamblers and infidels weeping their way to the Cross. Eventually many of these were baptized with the Holy Spirit and became members of the Church. About this time also many new churches were founded and eventually some eighty were established in South Wales, most of them with properties of their own.

In addition to Pastors D. P. Williams and T. Jones, Pastor T. Rees was called as an Apostle at a Pentecostal Convention at Tonypandy in 1921, through Pastor W. J. Williams. Pastor J. O. Jones was used to call Pastors W. H. Lewis and T. V. Lewis to the Apostleship in 1925. Pastor J. Purnell was also chosen for this office. Pastor D. P. Williams and these brethren journeyed through the valleys, confirming the faith of the members. A mighty work was done in Monmouthshire, in Aberdare Valley, the Rhondda, and in the Swansea and Llanelly areas.

In 1919 the Apostolic Church began a period of still greater advance. The work in Scotland, under the leadership of Pastor Andrew Turnbull, was linked with the work in Wales. Pastor Turnbull had a small assembly of Pentecostal believers in Glasgow. After hearing the ministry of the Pastors Williams in 1918 and 1919, they decided to join the Apostolic Church. In 1920, Pastor Turnbull was called to be an Apostle, his son, Tom, being a Prophet by his side. Since then over fifty assemblies have been opened in Scotland.

Pastor Frank Hodges, of Hereford, visited the Penygroes Convention in 1920 and invited the Welsh brethren to Hereford. They were astonished to find the words 'The Apostolic Church' on the notice board of the little assembly. At this time Pastor F. Hodges decided to have fellowship with the Apostolic Church. The work spread from Hereford to the Potteries, Birmingham, Plymouth and even Cornwall, many assemblies being opened.

For some years before this, there had been several groups around Bradford, called 'The Apostolic Churches of God,' with Pastor H. V. Chanter in charge of the work. He visited Apostolic Church Conventions in Wales and Scotland. In 1922, an invitation was sent to the leading brethren in Wales, Hereford and Scotland to attend the Convention at Bradford. The result was that the Bradford Churches also joined with the groups previously mentioned. So there came into existence in Great Britain one Apostolic Church. From Bradford, assemblies were opened in Yorkshire, Northumberland, Surrey and Kent.

At the Easter Conference of 1922, a small Executive was elected. It was comprised of Pastors D. P. Williams, A. Turnbull, H. V. Chanter and F. Hodges, with Pastor W. J. Williams serving as Prophet, to deal with any problems or difficulties that might arise between the four Sections which had been established. With the business of this central committee Pastors D. P. and W. J. Williams were closely connected.

At this same Conference the Apostolic Church Missionary Movement was born. The needs of overseas countries had not been overlooked by the Apostolic Churches in Wales. They had helped financially in sending Pastors Roderick and Brooks to South Africa.

In January, 1919, some forty overseers and elders met at Birchgrove, in the Swansea Valley, under the chairmanship of Pastor D. P. Williams. It was decided at this meeting that a missionary offering should be taken regularly in each assembly and sent to Penygroes. At Bradford prophetical ministry came through Pastor W. J. Williams and a united missionary movement was established in the British Isles, with Bradford as its centre. Thus the four Sections were united spiritually, doctrinally and in missionary enterprise.

Here is an excerpt from prophetical ministry given at that time : " I would have you to know that I am revealing My will concerning the missionary work. In unity I would have you to work in this matter. I would not have the three nations to raise each its own missionary work. I have those of My choice in the midst of the three nations, but you cannot send them if you are going to act separately. If you are willing for My plan, I will reveal it unto you. The centre of the work I would have to be in this place, Bradford, for a great purpose have I in this. Mark ye My word that those that are dark of skin shall rejoice for your gathering this night."

As a result of the missionary activities being united at this Conference, the first monthly Missionary Prayer Meeting of the whole Church was held on Monday evening, June 5, 1922. A Missionary Council was set up, members attending from Scotland, England and Wales. Large Conventions were arranged to be held in Glasgow, at the New Year, in Bradford at Easter, in Hereford at Whitsuntide, and in Penygroes during the week including the August Bank Holiday.

A magazine was launched from the Bradford Missionary Centre, under the editorship of Pastor H. V. Chanter. It has now been published for forty years, giving evangelical and missionary news. Pastor W. J. Williams was sub-editor for this magazine for a number of years. Missionary offerings have increased from £1,000 in 1922 to over £20,000 in 1961.

Controlled by the Missionary Committee in Great Britain, missionary work is conducted and supported in Nigeria, Ghana, the Cameroons, Dahomey, India, Italy, France, and Southern Rhodesia, the members numbering over 90,000 in 1963 in the countries mentioned. Under the Missionary Board in the South Pacific, the Board members being from the Apostolic Churches in Australia and New Zealand, missionary work is carried on in New Guinea, New Hebrides, among the Aborigines of Australia, and the Maoris of New Zealand. Under the Missionary Board of North America, the members of the Board being appointed from the Churches in Canada and U.S.A., missionary work has been established in the West Indies and among the Roman Catholics in Montreal. Under the Missionary Board in Denmark, missionaries have gone to China, Africa and Greenland. Apostles, Prophets and Pastors have also been sent to Australia, New Zealand, Canada, U.S.A., and to the Continent from the Mother Church in Great Britain to help establish Apostolic Churches in these lands. Although these countries are autonomous, spiritually and doctrinally they are joined with all the Apostolic Churches throughout the world.

In six countries in Europe over 200 assemblies have been established, many of them opened since World War II. Most are found in Denmark, Switzerland and Italy, but the work is growing steadily in Germany and France, and lately commenced in Holland. In Hungary, too, a sizeable group believing the same message has recently been contacted. Pastors D. P. and W. J. Williams played a major part in the progress of the missionary work.

They also travelled incessantly at home, expanding the work in Great Britain and strengthening the Churches. Other Apostles and Prophets, called into the full-time ministry, were likewise being mightily used by God to open new assemblies in many parts of Great Britain. In 1930 there were no fewer than 150 Apostolic Churches in the British Isles.

By 1934 there were seven " Sections," as they were called, in the United Kingdom. These seven Sections were united in 1937, making the Church one in a still more intimate way. In various Councils before that year it had been decided that

unity must be established in the Apostolic Church in Great
Britain. Prophetical ministry had come through a number
of the Prophets to this effect. Finally, certain brethren were
set aside to draft a Constitution and draw up Guiding
Principles. When the seven Sections became one, Penygroes
was selected as the General Headquarters, Bradford as the
Missionary Centre, and Glasgow as the Finance Centre.
Pastor D. P. Williams was the first President of the work.
Pastor H. Dawson was appointed Acting President, with
Pastors A. Turnbull and F. Hodges as Vice-Presidents. By
this time Pastor H. V. Chanter was superintending the work
in U.S.A. A Council of Apostles and Prophets was established, with a smaller body acting as an Executive. This
increased the burden of work on the Pastors Williams,
as Pastor D. P. Williams was Chairman of Council and
Executive meetings, and Pastor W. J. Williams took a major
share of the prophetical ministry.

The following is a statement made by Pastor D. P. Williams,
as Chairman of a convocation of Apostles and Prophets, at
the opening of the Council in October, 1929. This utterance
is recorded here because at that time the seven Sections of
the Church in Britain were contemplating union. Here it is :

" At the opening of this Council I feel timid and unequal
in facing the programme before us, but I am relying on your
prayers. The assemblies among the nations are expecting to
derive some benefit from these meetings, and we must do our
best not to disappoint them. While we are dealing with the
matters on our agenda it is very important for us to remain
in the Spirit of Christ. We should remember that He is at
the head of the table, and the tenor of our speech should
be on a plane that we would not be ashamed of in His
presence. We should remember that He is here amongst us,
as He was with His apostles and disciples of old, and therefore we should guard our hearts and spirits as far as possible.

In the discussion we should not strike one another with words, nor ignore one another in our debates."

"Again we should remember that we are not here that our own personal revelation should have the pre-eminence, but that everything suggested will be for the benefit of the Body of Christ at large. Neither should we speak from a national standpoint, for we are not here representing individual nations, but the Holy Nation, the Body of Christ. There is always a danger for the individual to bring in his own limited vision, and local views, instead of remembering that his little tributary should flow into a larger river. In such a convocation as this we must become one in vision, opinion, and revelation, until the national falls into the great international flow."

"There may be," continued the President, "in these meetings a higher plane of the good and perfect will of God for us. Over and over again in international gatherings like this the Holy Spirit has been throwing hints to the effect that He has further revelations of His Divine will for the Body at large, and saying that we are not ripened and matured in our faith and in our comprehensions for further revelations. I hope God will find every heart ready to receive the further will of God, even to the uttermost. We do not know what God has in store for us in these gatherings, but I pray that we may all be transformed in our spirits to receive what God has to reveal, whether through the wisdom of the Apostles, or through the Word of the Lord in these gatherings."

From 1921 to 1932 the International Convention of the Apostolic Church was held in the Memorial Hall, Penygroes, and each year it was mightily blessed by God. The Apostolic Temple was built and opened in Penygroes in 1933. This building has a capacity of 1,500 persons and was filled every year. The foundation stones have inscriptions in English and Welsh, the latter commemorating the Welsh Revival.

Solemn and ever to be remembered was the breaking of bread on that first Sunday morning in this new Temple. It brought God into the midst of the Convention as never before. Pastor D. P. Williams was an outstanding convener, and richly expounded the spoken word. The prophetical ministry through Pastor W. J. Williams was also deeply appreciated.

The two Pastors were likewise closely linked with the inauguration of the Apostolic Church Bible School at Penygroes the following year. Students attend this school from the British Isles, the Continent, and indeed from all over the world. The two Pastors gave lectures to the students, who received great benefit from them.

PART IV

DRAFTED OVERSEAS

CHAPTER SIX

JOURNEYS ABROAD

PASTORS D. P. and W. J. Williams journeyed together for twenty-three years, from 1922 to 1945, visiting many countries, always being sent forth through prophetical ministry. They visited Italy six times, Denmark four, France nine times, once they went to West Africa, once to Australia and New Zealand, and three times to Canada and U.S.A.

During their travels they had the privilege of leading people of over twenty nationalities to know the Lord Jesus Christ. Among those who were regenerated were Sinnfeiners, Atheists, Agnostics and Infidels. The visits also had much to do with the inaugurating and consolidating of the Apostolic Church in the countries through which they travelled.

Pastor T. Davies stated that Mr. T. Griffiths, brother of the Right Honourable James Griffiths, the well-known Labour leader, testified on the radio and in a South Wales newspaper to the world-wide influence of the Apostolic Church. This influence was made possible by the pioneering work of Apostles and Prophets, including the Missionary journeys of the Pastors Williams.

Northern Ireland

The first country to be opened up under the new Missionary Centre at Bradford was Northern Ireland. During 1919, prophetical ministry was given concerning Ireland, and about the possibilities of opening up a work in that country. A brother named Benjamin Fisher, of Belfast, was at the

Glasgow Convention of 1920. He invited the Williams brothers and others to visit Belfast to minister in that city. The result was a 14 day Mission held at the Orange Hall, Great Victoria Street. Of that Mission the only visible results were seen on the last Sunday when 35 souls were saved. Eventually, in Northern Ireland 87 accepted the right hand of fellowship.

Prophetical ministry came on this occasion that another party of twelve would come to Belfast. It was therefore decided to hold a Convention in Belfast in June. Riots broke out in the city, however, some people being killed. Because of this, many of the fifty visitors who intended travelling to Belfast cancelled their visit. The riots became so fierce and widespread that it was feared it would be impossible to hold the services as arranged, but a word came from the Lord that certain Pastors were to attend. The prophetic message was as follows : " Go thou, for I am the Lord of land and sea, and I will cause you to return to Penygroes with the first fruit of that land with you." When the Pastors arrived in Belfast it was found that exactly twelve had crossed the water, as the spoken word had promised. This confirmed the Irish members in the Apostolic vision. After a splendid Convention in Belfast, twenty-five members from that city came to the Penygroes Convention.

The Irish brethren now wrote to Pastor D. P. Williams, asking for a Pastor to come to Belfast to take charge of the work there. Prophetical ministry came through Pastor W. J. Williams saying Pastor W. Phillip was to be sent to Ireland. He took charge, and helped by other Pastors, established there a sound and healthy Apostolic Church. This is the prophetic word : " I call My servant Phillip from the little nation, to be sent forth to Ireland that I may work, indeed. Though they have been rebelling against one another, I have in that nation My choice. I would have you, my servant, to be willing to suffer, for if you will suffer with Me, you shall reign with Me."

North America

Pastors D. P. Williams and W. J. Williams visited America, along with Pastors A. Turnbull and F. Hodges in 1922. This was in response to a request from a Christian in America who, while on holiday in Scotland, had attended the Glasgow Church. During the Bournemouth Conference of August, 1913, the Holy spirit uttered the words, " Carmania, Carmania," through the lips of Pastor D. P. Williams. One of the Prophets present afterwards revealed that this was the name of a ship, and some who were present would sail on it to another land. It was fulfilled when the four Pastors sailed on the ' Carmania ' to U.S.A.

The four Pastors visited a group of Pentecostal Christians in East Lansdowne, Philadelphia. They encountered considerable opposition, but in spite of that they established there the first Apostolic Church in U.S.A. Travelling 3,000 miles throughout America and Canada, they preached to many Christians the Full Gospel, and were especially used in Toronto in preaching the Word.

Their ministry was instrumental in the elimination of many schismatic notions. Some were giving a too exalted place to the spoken word at the expense of the Written Word. A true balance was struck in that connection. Prophetical ministry on this occasion came that the Apostolic flame would continue to burn in Toronto. Since then the work in that city has continually shown evidence of the blessing of God. Everywhere they preached, the Pastors made a profound impression under the guidance of the Holy Spirit.

In time prophetical ministry came in East Lansdowne saying that one of the four Pastors would come back to visit them. In 1926 the Council of Great Britain sent Pastor

W. J. Williams to U.S.A. This encouraged the members in the Church in Philadelphia, knowing that the prophetic word previously given had literally come to pass. He ministered in East Lansdowne and Altoona with great power. Because of his labours under the unction of the Holy Spirit, the numbers attending the services increased and some who had left the fellowship returned, others received the baptism of the Holy Spirit, and contributions to the Church increased fourfold.

In another city the Pastor was asked to preach for three weeks, on the Tenets of the Church. He acceded to their request and at the end of the services there was great joy in the midst as many souls had been saved. Eighteen people joined the Apostolic Church, and took the right hand of fellowship. One of them was later called to be an Apostle.

In April, 1934, the two brothers paid a third visit to America. On this occasion they travelled nearly 5,000 miles in U.S.A. and Canada, preaching at most of the Apostolic assemblies. Many souls were saved and the ministry of the Written and Spoken Word was so penetrating that on occasions whole congregations were melted before God, the members dedicating themselves in His presence.

Both Pastors met in conclave many of the elders of the various assemblies, and the following is a summary of a statement made by Pastor D. P. Williams to the elders of Nova Scotia :

" It is a privilege to meet together in the same faith, with the object of consulting about it, and establishing one another in it, and to consider how to extend the faith universally. By the faith I mean not the mere belief in a system of truth, but the truth itself, in its embodiment. The full-orbed truth as it covers the vast field of divine revelation, delivered to apostles and prophets and communicated by them to others. The calling of elders and other officers is for the purpose that they may enrich themselves with that body of truth, so as to build up and make perfect those under their charge."

" The body of truth has been ordained for the members of the Body, the whole being built in harmony together by it. There is the possibility of being versed in the truth in one aspect, and yet neglecting some other aspect. Some are strong in theology, others on the devotional side, others on the evangelical or the practical ; but the Body of Christ needs the full body of truth, in order to be perfected. This requires us to have a deep knowledge of it, and especially a corresponding life behind all that is said. There is the possibility of neglecting the truth, because of the lack of a godly character. The truth suffers, and the members of the Church suffer because of this."

In 1939 Pastors D. P. Williams and J. O. Jones again visited Canada and America. They preached in many Apostolic Churches. Forty members of the Church met them when they arrived in Montreal, thus fulfilling the prophecy, made through Pastor W. J. Williams, that the next time Pastor D. P. Williams visited the city, there would be a company of God's people to meet him. The Church was filled at the services, and the ministry of the Word was so strong that many came out for consecration. After Pastor Williams had delivered his message to a French assembly in Montreal, twenty-eight were received into fellowship.

They then journeyed the 1,000 miles to Nova Scotia, ministering to the assemblies for nine days, from thence proceeding to Philadelphia, where the members of the church were having a difficult time, but the ministry of the Pastors miraculously changed the situation. Using Pastor H. V. Chanter's car, the two Pastors travelled 5,000 miles, visiting the assemblies in North America, and experiencing special blessing in every service.

Returning to Montreal, they were warmly received. At

the station, on their departure, a great crowd gathered to bid them Godspeed on their return journey to Britain. To the singing of ' Cwm Rhondda,' the Pastors set out for New York and so for home.

In 1945 Pastor D. P. Williams, accompanied by his wife, again travelled thousands of miles in North America. As a result, many were saved and whole families were added to the Church. He was clothed with the heavenly mantle of power and inspiration while preaching, and many were blessed spiritually. Some were healed, others baptized with the Holy Spirit, and in the Name of Jesus demons were cast out.

A notable event took place in Canada at this time. Autonomy was granted to the work in the Dominion. Also a North American Missionary Board was inaugurated.

Pastor D. P. Williams also visited the U.S.A. from Canada and attended the East Lansdowne Convention at Easter. He preached in many assemblies in U.S.A. and travelled hundreds of miles by train, car and bus. One Church in Baltimore was led to join forces with the Apostolic Church. Some thirty people were given the right hand of fellowship. Throughout his tour of North America, Mrs. Williams was to the Pastor an invaluable help and companion on the many long and arduous journeys.

The illness of their daughter, Mair, in Penygroes, was a heavy burden upon Pastor Williams and his wife on their American itinerary, but they were wonderfully sustained until the main object of their mission had been accomplished.

While in Toronto, a Church seating 1,000 people was rented. Large crowds attended the services, among them many ministers of the Full Gospel. During the meetings many of these ministers and other Christians were on their faces before God. Some of them later joined the Church. In due course the Pastor and his wife returned to their own beloved Wales.

Denmark

The revival which began in Wales in 1904 had echoes in Copenhagen in 1905. In 1912 a Miss Anna Larssen, who had been saved and baptized by the Holy Spirit, married Sigurd Bjorner, a Y.M.C.A. secretary in Denmark. They worked with the State Church until baptized in water in 1919. Afterwards they continued their work with a tent mission, first at Hellerup, and then at Trianglen, Copenhagen. At the end of the tent meetings in 1922, they erected 'Evangeliehuset,' or the Gospel House.

In 1922 a sister of the assembly visited the Penygroes Convention. She was so impressed that she persuaded Pastor Bjorner to attend the Convention the following year. The Holy Spirit witnessed in his heart to the Apostolic Church the moment he arrived at Penygroes, and he spoke with tongues. Afterwards prophetical ministry came through Pastor W. J. Williams calling him as an apostle and to minister the Full Gospel in Denmark, and the Pauline order of the Church polity. He returned home to find the self-same Spirit had made his call known in Copenhagen, and there was much rejoicing.

In 1924 Pastors D. P. Williams and W. J. Williams, along with others, visited Denmark. Meetings were held twice a day, and many leaders of Christian assemblies in Denmark, Norway and Sweden attended business meetings in the afternoons. Pastor D. P. Williams was called on to answer many interesting questions concerning the Apostolic vision. Here are some of the questions asked and the answers given.

One question was : " If an Apostle is separated in another country, without being anointed with oil, would he be acknowledged as an Apostle among you ?" Pastor D. P. Williams answered : " Oil is a symbol of the Holy Spirit, and a sign that God would endue the men anointed with the divine qualities necessary for their service. Yet the oil

does not make them apostles or elders, they are apostles in
the predestinations of God. It is also true that while it is
according to the harmony of the Scriptures, it is only
associated with ordination in the Old Testament." He
pointed out that many things done by Christian churches
were not mentioned in the New Testament, such as the
holding of Conventions, Sunday Schools, Young People's
Meetings, and so on. The use of musical instruments is not
mentioned in the New Testament. Pastor Williams added :
" At the time of a Convention in Wales, I was taken ill,
and was too weak to walk, and had to go to bed. I asked
an elder to anoint me. Then a voice came with divine
revelation in my soul saying, ' Arise, My servant, and wash
thyself in the bath in cold water.' I did not have any
Scripture for it in the New Testament, but I remembered
that Naaman of old went down seven times into the Jordan.
I obeyed God, and was able to attend my duties at the
Convention."

Replying to the query : " How are we to know when there
is a Prophet for the Body at large ?" he answered, " The way
that we know that they are elect of God is by the nature of
the prophecies that come through them, and the fact that
their prophecies are fulfilled. The Apostle Paul said : ' All
may prophesy,' but a Prophet in the Body is in the predestinations of God, and what comes through such a man
speaks for itself without any explanation."

February 6, 1924, was the day on which the members of
the assembly in Copenhagen were to decide whether or not
to join the Apostolic Church. All six hundred of them rose
and accepted the doctrines of the Church, which were quoted
from the "Riches of Grace," these being expounded by Pastor
D. P. Williams during his fortnight's stay in the city. From
that day forward the church in Denmark was known as the
Apostolic Church, its official magazine being the ' Evangelie-

bladet,' or ' Gospel News.' Since then the Danish Church has remained an integral part of the world Apostolic Church, and continued true to its tenets. Other Pentecostal assemblies in Kolding, Roskilde, Holbeck, Elsinor and Gillileje welcomed the Apostolic vision, while other assemblies asked to join later. Over the years, the work in Denmark has grown solidly, and as this book goes to press there are about sixty assemblies in that country.

During the week when the Danish Church was set in order meetings were held at the flat of Dr. Carl Naeser, and were addressed by Pastor D. P. Williams. The following are the names of some of the distinguished visitors present.

Her Ladyship the Over-Mistress of the Royal Court of H.M. Queen of Denmark.

Baronesse Marie Bille (Born Countess Moltke).

Kammerherreinde Bille (Born Countess Raben-Levetzau).

Etatsraadinde Gamel, also Commander V. Lorck and family.

Redaktor (Editor) Gulmar, (Chief Editor of the Denmark ' Times ').

Redaktor Poulson, of the Denmark ' Times.'

Kapt of Artillerie Rohde and Lady, also Dr. and Mrs. Vincent Naeser.

A number of the chief Sub-Editors of the daily paper, Denmark ' Times.'

Authoress IIngeborg Marie Sick, also Pastor and Mrs. Bjorner.

Chief Engineer Kristen Mollar, also Professorinde Anna Poulson.

Lutheran Pastor Mollerup, also Marchend en Gros Gad.

President of the Baptist Churches of Denmark, L. Jorgensen, and two other Pastors.

Auxilliary Brigade of the Salvation Army, twenty-five members.

It may be added that the Copenhagen ' Times ' published a prominent article concerning the visit of the two Pastors and party, with a photo of the President of the Church Council of Great Britain. Also during this fortnight prophetical ministry came through Pastor W. J. Williams, predicting the coming of the Second World War. The word said : " Europe will again be bathed in blood, and your country (Denmark) will not escape." How literally this prophetic message came to pass !

A few months later, Pastor D. P. Williams visited Denmark again, for a Bible Study Week which had been specially arranged for his visit. The Bible Readings by the Pastor were very helpful, and of an extraordinary value for the building up of the Church as a whole.

In the middle of the week a fast was proclaimed. The Holy Spirit brooded over the people in a special way with the result that many were healed. One was cured of a spinal disease, another of rupture, a third of a fever and a fourth of peritonitis. Others were healed spiritually. One testified : " I have been delivered from secret sin." Another : " I came with an angry and quarrelsome spirit, but now I am free from it."

In 1925 another visit was paid to Denmark by Pastors W. J. Williams and H. V. Chanter. The congregations listened with great interest and joy to the addresses of the brethren. The theme of the Conference was ' Oneness,' and the theme continued to be that throughout. The whole of Saturday was given over to prayer. In the evening a meeting was held with all the leaders of the Church in Denmark, about sixty persons being present. There were no problems. Apostolic principles and practices were acceptable to all. Pastor W. J. Williams was used as a prophet to reveal God's plan for certain brethren. On the Sunday night those called were set apart into office.

When Pastors D. P. Williams and A. Turnbull visited Denmark, the large church at Copenhagen was crowded to capacity. They also undertook a 3,000 kilometer motor-car tour, being received everywhere with great joy. There were large audiences in most places and their ministry was of immense value in the building up of the Church.

The leader of the Hillerod Church had a son who was demon possessed. The father could not, either by persuasion or discipline, prevent him from stealing, lying, and swearing. The lad was so audacious that he actually stole from his father's pocket while being chastised. The Pastors talked with the boy, and as they prayed for him, the boy himself shouted : " Go, Devil !" The demon went out of him, and he was transformed from that moment. In another place, Naestved, although some tarried for the baptism of the Holy Spirit they did not receive it. However, on the way home a whole company in a motor-car were baptized, speaking with tongues as the Holy Spirit gave them utterance.

In 1930 Pastors D. P. Williams and W. A. C. Rowe visited Denmark, and the ministry of the Written Word was greatly blessed, with the result that many souls were saved. After Bible Readings for the deepening of spiritual life, many of God's people consecrated themselves afresh to God. It was during this visit that it pleased the Lord to reveal His choice of four apostles in the Body of Christ, and these were duly set apart to this calling.

In 1935 the Pastors Williams visited Copenhagen and ministered in the Headquarters Church. The feast of spiritual truths was rich, God revealing to the listeners His purpose for these latter days. Nine souls responded to the call of God on the Sunday night.

Norway

The Pastors afterwards visited Oslo, Norway's capital.

In a service attended by some eight hundred people real Pentecostal power was manifested. At one meeting Pastor W. J. Williams preached for one hour ; and, after he finished, coffee was served, but this was only a break. The Pastors thought it was the end of the service, but the leaders said : " Another hour now." Pastor D. P. Williams then addressed the audience and preached with mighty power, the Lord working with him.

Estonia

In 1934 Pastor D. P. Williams visited Estonia. He made a second visit a year later. He was given a warm welcome on both occasions. The Scriptures were expounded, and the tide of revival rose higher and higher. Many souls sought and found pardon and peace. Eventually there were twenty-five assemblies in fellowship with the Apostolic Church in Estonia, but the war put an end to this contact. Today these churches are behind the Iron Curtain.

All the visits of the Pastors Williams to the various countries mentioned were attended by great blessing and power, bringing much help to the members of the Church, as well as to others.

CHAPTER SEVEN

MORE JOURNEYS ABROAD

IN this chapter we again follow the brethren on their travels abroad. When Pastor D. P. Williams was welcomed back to Penygroes after an absence of ten years, having in the meantime held pastorates in Pontypridd and Skewen, South Wales, he said : " It is humanly impossible to describe the last ten years of the work away from Penygroes, the difficulties, the journeys oft, nearly 50,000 miles in thirteen lands." During that time he preached the Gospel to representatives of many countries and had among other privileges that of pointing an Arab to the Saviour. Arabs, as we know, are not easily won to Christ.

France

While Pastors D. P. and W. J. Williams were in Denmark in 1924, prophetical ministry indicated that God desired that they should visit Paris. Along with Pastor Naeser, the two brothers went there, where a few eager Christians gathered to hear them. In these services some were saved and backsliders were restored. Pastor Naeser acted as interpreter throughout the meetings. During this visit he received the baptism of the Holy Spirit and spoke with tongues, the tongue being interpreted by Pastor W. J. Williams. Before the brothers left for Wales, he handed them a souvenir gift of 1,000 kroner for the Church in Wales, stipulating that the money was to be used to help pay for an Open-air Baptistery.

Here is an extract from the prophetical ministry through Pastor W. J. Williams concerning France : " Inasmuch as I have said that ye should ask for a new mission field, ask for that nation France, that ye may enter therein. I cannot be leaf to the cry of the righteous." It was not long afterwards

73

that missionaries were called for France, and the work in that country commenced. Since then the work has slowly but surely advanced and there are a number of Apostolic assemblies in that country.

The two brothers were again in Paris in 1929, when the room in Rue Serandoni was packed, a number of nations being represented. There were Christians from various Protestant denominations, as well as a few missionaries who were training in Paris. Five souls were saved and others were baptized in the Holy Spirit. Seven were also baptized in water. On one of their visits to France, the two Pastors were given a hostile reception from the people of Aignan, but were able to escape without injury.

Returning to France in 1930, Pastor D. P. Williams was encouraged to see fifteen souls deciding for Christ and ten being received into the Church. There was, too, evidence of God's healing power at work during this visit.

The Pastor set foot in France yet again in 1931, along with Pastors A. Turnbull and F. Hodges, and large numbers attended the services to hear them. Twenty-five were saved and many healed. The gatherings were large, and, after the Pastors had left, the first prayer meeting was attended by seventy people, thanking God for the visitation.

Pastors D. P. and W. J. Williams and H. Croudson visited the Apostolic assemblies in France in 1933, and the ministry was beneficial to the hearers. In the same year, Pastor D. P. Williams and others were again in Paris, and every assembly visited was enriched in life and power. He preached to three different assemblies in Paris, and thirty souls were saved. On a Friday evening nearly four hundred people attended and eight souls were saved, and one person was delivered from the domination of a demon.

The two Pastors, when travelling in continental countries, had at times difficulty in making themselves understood. On one occasion they were in a café for lunch. Pastor D. P. Williams ordered fried eggs for both, but the waiter could not understand. Finally his brother Jones crowed like a cockerel, and made the actions of breaking an egg, and the noise of an egg frying. The waiter understood, and they obtained their fried eggs.

Italy

A prophetic word given through Pastor W. J. Williams in a Penygroes Convention said : " In My movements in the Church, I am not only moving you to the uncivilized world in regard to the missionary cause, I am making a direct move in the Body of the Apostolic Church towards and against the ' Great Babylon.' I am revealing to you that My battle is against the ' Great Whore ' at the end of the age."

At the beginning our missionaries were always sent to the countries steeped in Roman Catholicism, such countries as Ireland, Argentine, Italy and France. God declared in this prophecy that the work of the Body of Christ is to counteract the work of the Woman spoken of in the Book of Revelation. The centre of this vast movement being in Italy, God sent His servants there to open a work.

By invitations, in February, 1927, the Pastors Williams along with some brethren from Denmark visited the Italian Apostolic Church at Civita Vecchia. At Grosseto a group of believers intimated their desire to join the Apostolic Church, and two brothers were separated as elders. In time a fine hall was built there, and the assembly flourishes to this day. In Civita Vecchia thirty souls were saved and many were healed. Most of the listeners in Grosseto were Roman Catholics, but they paid heed to the message, and twenty-six gave themselves to the Lord.

The Pastors visited the Pantheon, the temple of the heathen gods of pagan Rome, now the burial place of the Kings of Italy. They also visited the Colosseum, where Christians had so often been martyred. The amphitheatre once held over fifty thousand spectators, a special part being partitioned off for the Kings of many centuries ago, and the Nobles of that time. Those kings and nobles gazed at the most bloody atrocities, the cruel, hungry beasts, rushing out to devour the Christians amid the cheers and execrations of the hostile throng of spectators. The Pastors left this place with memories that would last.

They looked over the Vatican, where the Pope, at that time, was virtually a prisoner in the Vatican City, and visited the Church of St. Peter, with its fabulous high altar and wonderful mural decorations. They paid a visit to the dark dungeon, deep in the earth, where Paul is said to have been imprisoned along with forty criminals. Not far distant, it is said, is the spot where he was martyred.

The catacombs, tunnelled under the earth for hundreds of miles, engaged their special interest, owing to their association with the fate of the early Christians of Rome. Here the Christians lived like moles, in fear of their lives, yet enjoying the peace of God in their hearts. Small temples were made in which to worship God, and here they were hunted, killed, and buried.

In 1928 the Pastors Williams paid a return visit to Italy, preaching in the churches already mentioned and also to a small group which had gathered in a house in Rome. This they counted a great privilege, to preach the Gospel, like Paul, in Rome. In 1930 Pastors W. J. Williams, A. Turnbull and F. Hodges officiated at the opening of the Grosseto Hall. In the services forty-two souls were saved and many were healed of a variety of afflictions. Other assemblies were also visited, the Lord performing signs and wonders in each place and many being saved. In Rome nearly fifty people gave their hearts to Christ.

In 1933 a further visit was paid by the Pastors Williams

and Pastor H. Croudson, who was at that time Missionary Secretary. They were accorded a joyful welcome when they visited the Grosseto and Civita Vecchia assemblies. In Rome they ministered with great effect. On their last night there, the Church was set in order in that city. An elder and a deaconess were called, and eleven came out to receive the right hand of fellowship.

Missionaries from the church in Great Britain were sent to Italy and, in spite of Roman Catholic opposition, the work was extended to various parts of the country. Today, throughout the country, there are nearly fifty assemblies.

Nigeria

In 1931 correspondence with the African leaders of a church called the ' Faith Tabernacle,' led to a request for a delegation comprised of some of the leaders of the Apostolic Church, Great Britain, to visit Nigeria, where the Lord had already begun a great work. During the Whitsuntide Council Meetings in Hereford in 1931, it was decided that Pastors D. P. Williams, W. J. Williams and A. Turnbull should go out to Nigeria. They left Liverpool in September of that year.

It was through copies of our church magazine the " Riches of Grace " reaching West Africa that the request was made. Thus was established a link between the two churches. On board ship, the R.M.S. " Adda," a meeting was held at which some fifty Africans were present. On the last night of the voyage, forty natives were on their knees, taking Christ as Saviour.

On reaching Lagos the three Pastors were greeted by Pastor D. O. Odubango, and many West African pastors and elders. A great reception was held, the building being packed to capacity. Many leaders had come from the hinterland, and some from as far afield as the Gold Coast, now known as Ghana. Among those present were Pastors Adeboyega and

Sakpo, who are two of the present leaders of the Apostolic
Church in the Western, Northern and Lagos Areas of Nigeria.

The visitors were kept very busy every day, large numbers
coming for healing and prayer.   On the first Sunday morning
the church was crowded, some four hundred and fifty people
being present.   Elders' meetings were held on two nights,
when arrangements were made for a fortnight's services to
be conducted in the capital city of Lagos.   In these services
the power of God was mightily manifest, the services con-
tinuing for over two weeks, with more than fifty people being
anointed daily for divine healing.   Many bore witness to
deliverance from bodily ailments.   The congregations reached
such numbers that many had to listen through the windows.
During the campaign in Lagos nearly four hundred souls
were saved, many were healed and many received the baptism
of the Holy Spirit.

The hall was crammed with enthusiastic congregations.   In
spite of the intense heat, the delegation were able to minister
with great power.   Near the end of the mission at Lagos,
another hall next to the Mission building had to be hired to
accommodate the crowds.

The " Nigerian Press " of Lagos reported :   " Never before
has Lagos witnessed such scenes as those now daily taking
place in this Divine Healing and Revival Campaign.   Every
night hundreds seek salvation from sin, and the baptism of
the Holy Spirit.   Many have testified to the healing power
of Christ in their body.   That the days of miracles are not
past is being proved every morning and evening in these
meetings since the Revival started.   The Revivalists hold it
essential thoroughly to instruct people as to the teaching of
the Word of God as a basis of their faith.   The essential
part of the meetings is soul-winning.   Divine healing comes
second.   They do not in any way attempt to discredit the
value of healing, but the first is vitally essential."

" The Revivalists maintain that Pentecost is the condition of all true service to God. The pre-eminent promise of the Bible to God's children is His promise to baptize them with the Holy Spirit. They say that the greatest blow the devil ever gave the Church was when he made people teach that all men are baptized with the Holy Spirit at regeneration. It has robbed millions of Christians of the spiritual gifts of the Holy Spirit, and has kept them from finding their place in the Body of Christ."

After the special services at Lagos, a tour of other churches connected with this body of African believers was undertaken. Centres were chosen for the holding of Conventions, and a special itinerary was made for the Pastors in Nigeria, ministry being given at Lagos, Tjebu-Ode, Abeokuta, Ibadan, Ilesha, Owo, Kaduna and Freetown. They also visited native Kings, and political officers in several places, which was helpful to the local churches. On a Saturday morning, travelling by boat, lorry, and finally by car, they reached Abege, their destination, to be greeted by a procession led by Pastor Esinsinade.

The same results were achieved at all the centres visited as in Lagos. Large crowds attended, with many being converted, healed and baptized in the Holy Spirit. One man afflicted by palsy in his leg was seen to throw away his crutches and walk. A church leader was cured of eye trouble, and others were relieved of their physical burdens.

The delegation visited Ikenna, afterwards named Ijebu Ode. With the help of an interpreter, the Gospel was preached with power, and some three hundred anxious enquirers were dealt with for salvation. The church hall was crowded, many failing to gain admittance. At Abeokuta an audience was given by the native King, the Alake, an educated and wise ruler. At the revival meeting held that evening, the Alake, his court and over a thousand of his subjects composed the congregation. About forty gave their hearts to the Lord, and on the following Monday twenty more were saved.

Proceeding to Ibadan, they saw the ruler, the Bale, who gave them premission to hold services. One of the persons present was the native Pastor, I. B. Akinyele, who is now himself the Bale of Ibadan, the largest town in Nigeria. The Pastors encouraged the natives to be patriotic and loyal British subjects, and entreated the congregations everywhere to be loyal to the Government authorities in accordance with the Scriptures. The representatives of the British Government received the visitors with kindness. A mighty outpouring of of the Holy Spirit showed that the favour of God was with the visitors in a special way. Thousands of natives came to the services, many being saved and healed.

In and around the town of Ilesha, the church members were refusing to pay the Poll Tax, claiming that the Lord was their King. Because of this some of the leaders had been arrested and imprisoned. After being instructed by the Pastors from Great Britain, and shown the authority of the Scriptures, they agreed to pay. The leaders were set free, and the Government officials were impressed, realising that the Pastors had achieved what they had been unable to do, and this incident created kindly feeling towards future missionaries.

Returning to Lagos, they met representatives of the church from various parts of Nigeria, and spent a fruitful fortnight discussing with open Bible matters of vital importance such as Church government, gifts of the Holy Spirit, Divine healing, polygamy, family life, communion, membership, baptism in water and ordinations. A foundation was laid for unity, and the African leaders decided that they should unite with the Apostolic Church. The Nigerian assemblies wholeheartedly embraced the Apostolic revelation, its principles and practices. This was the beginning of a great Apostolic work in West Africa, a revival movement which is still flourishing after thirty years.

Today there are over fourteen hundred churches in Nigeria, over one hundred and twenty in Ghana, and the work is still expanding. There are hundreds of full-time ministers in West Africa and also a good number of missionaries.

Through prophetical ministry, Pastor W. J. Williams gave a warning to future generations. At an earlier conference of the General Council at Bradford the Holy Spirit said through him : " At a future day the children of Ham will turn upon the children of Shem and Japhet, who are in occupation of Africa, and the conflict will be appalling." That word is being fulfilled at this moment.

On this, Pastor C. Rosser comments : " It needs little amplification to remind readers of the various risings in many parts of Africa, particularly in the Congo. Nevertheless, what consolation it must be to realize that Nigeria has entered into her independence and self governing status without bloodshed. Who knows what a glorious part the Gospel of Christ has played in this by showing its peaceful approach to each and every problem." Meanwhile what must be done is to redouble every effort evangelically, so that Africa's harvest of the redeemed may be increased.

Australia

The work in Australia, which has been so fruitful, began in Perth, West Australia, and soon spread to many other cities. The membership grew in Perth, Adelaide and Melbourne, and Pastors were sent out from Great Britain to shepherd the assemblies. As the result of a series of Revival Campaigns, over thirty assemblies were established in Australia in four years. The unwearied efforts of the original pioneering Pastors bore much fruit. Some of the main leaders must be named.

They were Pastors W. Cathcart, A. Gardiner, W. A. C. Rowe, J. Hewitt, J. McCabe, J. F. D. Thompson and A. Tate.

An invitation to the Pastors Williams to visit Australia was responded to in September, 1933, when they sailed from Britain. Arriving at Fremantle, they were welcomed by members of the Apostolic Church in Perth, after which they voyaged across the Australian Bight to Adelaide and thence to Melbourne. During their visit they travelled about the sub-continent visiting the widely dispersed assemblies. On reaching home, Pastor D. P. Williams said they had covered some forty thousand miles, slept in seventy different beds, and sometimes on floors when beds were not available, and sailed in nine different liners. They preached the Word constantly throughout the long journey.

The Centenary of the city of Melbourne was celebrated in the years 1933-4, and the visit of the two Pastors coincided with this great event. Innumerable visitors poured into Melbourne daily from all parts of the world. Accordingly, it was an opportune time for a Convention. Five hundred members gave the Pastors an enthusiastic reception at the first service which took the form of a great welcome tea. In the evening seven hundred people attended, and a choir sang an anthem composed in honour of the visitors, entitled : " We welcome you, our Ambassadors." The power of the Holy Spirit was demonstrated in many coming to Christ for salvation and in the healing of minds and bodies. Meetings were held daily, hundreds attending.

There is no sweeter time to an Apostolic member than that spent around the Lord's Table, and on this occasion the members of the congregation found themselves drawn right into the heavenly places. After a period of worship prophetical ministry came through Pastor W. J. Williams. How near God seemed to be, as the words of edification, exhortation, comfort and guidance were given, and in a deeper way than ever before His Headship was realized by those present, especially as He revealed His plans for the future of the work in that country. Then followed a wonderful exposition of the Spoken Word by the President. An outstanding feature of the Convention was the series of lectures given by the Pastors, on the history of the Apostolic Church, interwoven with the story of their own lives.

From Melbourne they went on to New South Wales and held services in the Sydney and Cessnock mining areas. The Apostolic work in Brisbane recently opened by Pastor J. H. Hewitt was visited, then on they went to New Zealand, finally returning to Melbourne. Afterwards they held highly successful missions in Adelaide and Perth. Even now, twenty-eight years later, there are those who talk of the blessings received under the ministries of the brothers Williams. The work done was both personal and general.

Here is one incident that took place during their journeys in the South Pacific. A man sent a message by a deacon that he wished to speak to the visitors. When he met them he said : " If there be a God, tell Him to save me, for I have been living in sin." " My brother and I will show you the way to obtain peace," said Pastor D. P. Williams. They spoke kindly to him in regards to repentance and faith in Christ, and three times he went on his knees, but he was too agitated to remain there. He rose and cried : " He cannot save me, I am damned already. I am going out, but where shall I go ? To hell in the end !" The Pastor asked him, " Who is your mother ?" " She is a deaconess in the Apostolic Church," he answered, " and I could not bear her prayers. I ran away from home," he said, falling again on his knees weeping. Suddenly a change came over him, as he realized that God had saved him. He then said : " I have never had such joy and peace before."

It was during their visit to Australasia that the Missionary

Advisory Board for the Church in Australia and New Zealand was set up. As a result, Mission fields were opened in India, China and Japan. Because of the 1939-45 war and the rise of Communism, the Chinese and Japanese fields were closed, and India came under the Missionary Committee of Great Britain. In time new fields were opened in New Guinea, New Hebrides, among the Maoris in New Zealand and the Aborigines in Australia. And over the years the work among these natives has made good progress.

New Zealand

When the brothers visited New Zealand they received a very warm welcome from the Pastors in that country and the members of the assemblies there. The work in this country was growing and prospering. The word preached through both the Pastors, and the prophetical ministry through Pastor W. J. Williams strengthened the work spiritually, doctrinally and practically.

Prophetical ministry came at the first service in Auckland, in words gracious, comforting, uplifting and encouraging. It was a wonderful new experience to many present. The prophetic word was received with awe and joy, as the people realized that, of a truth, God still speaks to His people. As they listened, time seemed to cease to be, and they dwelt at the threshold of Heaven itself. Pastor D. P. Williams gave an exposition of the Spoken Word, making clear to the minds of the congregations every point, driving home to their hearts matters of the deepest importance. Large numbers attended at the following services, visitors coming from many parts of the country.

The train journey to Wellington occupied fifteen hours through rich and varied scenery. Special services were held there and in other places visited, where their ministry was greatly appreciated ; nor did they spare themselves on their travels, but preached unweariedly the full Gospel of Christ, being remarkably sustained throughout.

India

On their way back to Britain they paid a visit to India. Miss M. Clark and some lady helpers were stationed in Poona, and there were stations in Ahmednagar and Kalhapur. A number of converts were baptized in water on this occasion. The Pastors preached the Gospel in these assemblies and this was deeply appreciated. At the close of one service, they were adorned with garlands of flowers as a token of friendship on the part of the Indians.

Since then the centre of the Indian work has been moved to Madras. In 1951 Pastor and Mrs. McCullough were sent out to take charge of the field. This was the signal for a forward move, and there are now a good number of Apostolic members in that country. In 1960 Pastor and Mrs. T. Stephens went out to help with the work, and their presence and ministry have also been a means of much blessing.

CHAPTER EIGHT

SUBSEQUENT ADVANCEMENT

AS a result of God laying His hand on the Williams brothers and others, the Apostolic Church has been established in over twenty countries. Their pioneering work, aided by other servants of God, has resulted in the coming into being of a world-wide organism. They have been instrumental, directly and indirectly, in bringing the peace and joy of the spiritual home to literally thousands of souls.

This seems all the more remarkable when we realize this great work commenced in a very small village. A small seed produces a great tree and from a very small village the great tree of the Apostolic Church has grown. It is very wonderful when one reads God's Word to see how insignificant places and people have been used by God to commence a great work. Penygroes, Carmarthenshire, South Wales, is one of those places, a place on God's roll of honour.

God touched the five continents through Pastor D. P. Williams and Pastor W. J. Williams from the little village of Penygroes. Wherever they went, the Lord worked with them, confirming the word with signs following. As a result of their work, and the work of other apostles, prophets and pastors, people have come to Penygroes, and especially to the Convention, from Norway, Denmark, Sweden, Germany, Italy, France, Switzerland, Holland, Australia, New Zealand, India, Canada, America, Nigeria, Ghana, South Africa, Southern Rhodesia and other countries. An Apostolic Church Bible College has been built at Penygroes, and students have come to it from Denmark, Switzerland, Italy, Germany, America, South Africa, and all parts of Great Britain. Many of the students have become ministers in the Apostoli

Church. All this has been possible since the Apostolic Church has been established in Scotland, England, Ireland, Wales, Canada, U.S.A., the West Indies, Denmark, Norway, France, Germany, Italy, Switzerland, Holland, Southern Rhodesia, South Africa, Nigeria, Ghana, Cameroons, Dahomey, Australia, New Zealand, New Hebrides, New Guinea, and India.

The two Pastors, in their day, had a large part in the work, which resulted in this remarkable progress. Much of the spade work was done by them, pioneering in very difficult fields. We do well to esteem and respect their memory in that they laboured much, as also did others at the beginning of the work.

There are many qualities which account for the outstanding achievements of these two servants of God. Primarily, they believed in the fundamentals of the Christian faith, adhering to the first principles of the Gospel, such as belief in the Triune God, the Divine Authority and Inspiration of the Holy Scriptures, the Deity, the Virgin Birth, Sinless Life, Atoning Death, and the Triumphant Resurrection of Christ. They believed that Christ and the Cross of Christ must always be to the fore and must always be preached.

Another factor which made them so outstanding in their work was their understanding of the truth concerning the Church, which is His Body, and their belief that the Ascension Gifts are for today, holding strongly in faith to the spoken word through the prophets. Pastor D. P. Williams was a theologian, who understood the depths of Christian doctrine and who took the full Gospel to the Christian. It was he who opened to us first of all the glories of the Apostolic order and vision. Furthermore, Pastor W. J. Williams was the first prophet used for the spoken word after the Apostolic Church was established.

There is no doubt that these two men were sent from God

with a message for this age, concerning the Body of Christ, Church government by apostles and prophets, and the other Ascension gifts, also the nine gifts of the Holy Spirit, together with their method of operation and use in the Church.

Their faithfulness, too, in these early years goes far to explain their success. When Pastor D. P. Williams was ill in Penygroes shortly before his death, he sent to the General Council, then in session in Bradford, asking for a word from the Lord. The prophetic word came through Pastor E. T. Edwards: "In life and in death, I have been with My servant, and am still with him. I gave him Apostleship. It has been retained. No one has been able to take his crown. My word again is, He has kept the faith under adverse circumstances, and through painful experiences, but no one can know of the preservation of faith like unto your God, saith the Lord."

Pastors D. P. Williams and W. J. Williams have passed away, but God has raised up others to continue their work. It is put clearly in the following verse repeated by Pastor V. Wellings at the funeral service of Pastor D. P. Williams.

The work is finished, a leader has gone,
    A challenge confronts us, we must carry on,
Great days are before us, unseen and unknown,
    Faith marches triumphant, God's still on the throne,
He will appoint others to lead in the fray,
    So let us be brothers till the great Crowning Day.

We should be imbued with the spirit of the Christian who said : " With all my discouragements and despondency, in my better moments I can think of no work worth doing compared with this. Had I a thousand lives, I would willingly spend them in it, and had I as many sons, I would gladly devote them to it."

As Pastor J. O. Jones said at Pastor D. P. Williams's funeral service : " Through our beloved Apostle's ministry, these deep truths, concerning the gifts of the ascended Christ, and the gifts of the Holy Spirit have been planted in our hearts, so that we have an urge within us that we shall not allow these truths to be forgotten, nor allow the manifestation of God's gifts in the Church to cease. We are going to keep the work going, the chariot wheels must roll on. We have lost our President, but we have not lost our Lord ! Let us therefore as Church officers and members follow faithfully in his footsteps."

It was a fitting coincidence that the Apostolic Church should celebrate the twenty-fifth Anniversary of its Missionary Movement in the year (1947) that Pastor D. P. Williams passed away, for both brothers were so closely linked with it. The following is a record of twenty-five years of Missionary endeavour by the Apostolic Church. In 1922, the missionary work began in U.S.A. In 1923, in Denmark ; 1924, China ; 1925, France ; 1927, Italy ; 1928, Canada ; 1930, Australia ; 1931 saw the turn of Nigeria ; 1932, Tasmania ; 1933, New Zealand ; 1934, India ; 1934, Estonia ; 1936, Japan ; 1937, Gold Coast, now called Ghana ; 1938, South Africa ; 1945, Norway ; 1946, Germany and Switzerland ; and the New Hebrides in 1947. All this in spite of the hindrance the work suffered because of the 1939-45 War.

There was a day, and that not so long ago, when the personnel on mission fields hardly outnumbered the administrative staff at the Missionary Centre. Yet within the brief space of twenty-five years the work has developed greatly.

At the outset God promised through prophetical ministry that if the Church members remained faithful, there would be no lack of finance. This promise has been abundantly fulfilled. Through the liberal giving of God's people, about one hundred persons had been sent to countries abroad up to 1947. In addition the Missionary Committee has paid the many other heavy expenses of the Missionary Movement, including furlough coverage, equipment needed on the Mission Field, fares and other items.

Since 1947 the Apostolic Church has continued to expand to a still greater extent. In 1920 the Apostolic Church could claim only some fifty assemblies. In 1930 the number had risen to about one hundred and fifty in Britain and a further fifty abroad. By 1947 there were one thousand two hundred and fifty assemblies throughout the world. By 1962 this number had risen to well over two thousand.

If this book proves anything, in the light of the current situation, it is that another revival is needed. Not a Welsh Revival merely, but a world revival. We should therefore pray that God will raise up amongst us more men of faith, loyalty, and dedication, like the early founders of the Church. Of themselves men are nothing, but God makes them sufficient for all the tasks He requires of them. It is His sufficiency which explains the amazing growth of the Apostolic Church in the brief period of forty years. God made His servants in the past equal to the tasks they had to undertake. He can make equal to His purposes any one, man or woman, who is willing to serve as an instrument of divine love and purpose.

PART V

ON PARADE

CHAPTER NINE

MINISTERIAL CALLING

IN the next three chapters a still more personal picture of Pastors D. P. Williams and W. J. Williams will be drawn. This chapter will deal with the ministerial calling of the two brothers.

PREACHING

At the outset of their ministry, both Pastor D. P. Williams and Pastor W. J. Williams preached in the Welsh language, but when they had to travel to other parts of the country, they found it necessary to express themselves in English. Burdened with duties, and Pastor D. P. Williams with a weak body, yet they remembered the last injunction of their blind father, William Williams, who said : " Never give in." So, by determination and patience, they mastered the English tongue.

Both brothers were prophetically directed to study the written Word, and they did so, becoming well versed in the knowledge of the Scriptures.

Pastor D. P. Williams, a reliable teacher, was also a splendid preacher. He spoke tellingly and with immense conviction. He was mightily used of God to establish the members of the Church in the doctrines of the Bible, as set forth in the Tenets of the Apostolic Church. His sermons have left an indelible impression on many people in many nations. Reading his sermons published in the " Riches of

Grace " reveals something of his power in this field.

He often spoke of the Cross life, death union with Christ, and holiness of life. This dynamic factor in his ministry serves to reveal the secret of his life-giving power. He did his utmost to inspire in the hearts of his hearers the attributes that would make them Christlike.

At the commencement of his Pontypridd pastorate he said, to members assembled at the Annual Christmas Convention in the Y.M.C.A. Hall : " The Lord has gathered His people, and I hope the little band that has been baptized in Ponty-pridd will be an honour to His Name. There are many large crowds in churches, but whether the Apostolic Church has large crowds or not, I desire members who will be wholly on the altar of God, people who will show forth the excellences and character of God." Such preaching excited in many hearts a desire for a sanctified life.

Pastor D. P. Williams also proclaimed the Government of the Lord Jesus Christ in and over His Church. He made known in five continents the doctrine of the Head of the Church. This is one of the main doctrines which has kept the Apostolic Church in being and unity during the last forty years. On the day of his funeral, the Bible lay open on Pastor D. P. Williams's coffin at Ephesians 4, which contains the divine truths that so firmly gripped his heart. He had preached the Full Gospel, and received a remarkable degree of revelation of Christ as Head of the Church.

Pastor W. J. Williams is also remembered as a most able and persuasive preacher. His single aim was to place the truth uncompromisingly before his hearers. His sermons were always impressive and inspiring, challenging and comforting Many will recall vividly his sermon on the ' Four Hallelujahs in the Book of Revelation.

His ministry was often strongly evangelistic, and he had a great desire to see souls saved. An unflagging contender fo

Pastor W. J. Williams later in life

William and Esther Williams "my great "
Grand parents

Pastor D. P. Williams later in life

Group of Apostolic Ministers attending
Penygroes Convention in early years

the faith delivered, once and for all, to the saints, he yet was also evangelical in his ministry.

When visiting an assembly in America he was opposed by much prejudice, because strong statements had been made in the past against the teachings of the Apostolic Church. His hearers were cold and indifferent, and he was broken-hearted, for there seemed no move from God. He decided to fast, and spent one morning wrestling with God, saying repeatedly: " Lord, you must save one soul tonight." That night, while preaching, he lost the thread of his message. Yet there was harmony in his heart, and he was inspired to sing. He obeyed the prompting, singing :

> O, why won't you come, in simple trusting faith,
>   Jesus will give you rest ?
> O happy rest, sweet happy rest,
>   Jesus will give you rest,
> O why won't you come in simple, trusting faith ?
>   Jesus will give you rest.

He sang this twelve times, the congregation being very bewildered. He was still singing when the door opened, a tall man entered, went to the front and fell on his knees. Later he said he had lived opposite the hall for sixteen years and had never been saved, but on this night, while in his kitchen, he heard Pastor W. J. Williams singing, and went to his front room to escape the voice. Still it pursued him throughout every room in the house, until he felt he had to respond to the plea. To the Pastor he said : " It has taken God to bring a little man like you to bring me to the Saviour." The cloud in the meeting was dissipated, and the glory came down. Afterwards, in every meeting, souls were saved.

AUTHORSHIP

Both brothers were writers as well as preachers. Pastor

D. P. Williams wrote in English and Welsh. He enriched Welsh hymnody with many hymns, many of them being contained in "Molwch Dduw," the Apostolic Welsh Hymnal. Of his English hymns a few are found in "Redemption Hymnal," in use in Apostolic and Pentecostal Churches.

His books include "The Prophetical Ministry," "The Work of an Evangelist" and "The Sanctuary of the Christian Life," all being greatly appreciated. Some of his editorials, sermons and articles published in "Riches of Grace" and "Apostolic Herald" have been reproduced in Canadian, Australian, New Zealand and Danish national magazines with wide acceptance.

No doubt Pastor D. P. Williams accomplished more in writing than did his brother, Jones, who was used primarily as a prophet. Pastor W. H. Lewis said at the funeral service of Pastor W. J. Williams : " Some men have been great scientists, and others great politicians, and some have been great preachers, but Pastor W. J. Williams was ordained as a prophet for the nations. Some members of the church may forget his sermons, but they will never forget the outstanding prophetical words that came through his lips." Yet there are to be found in the " Riches of Grace " and the " Apostolic Herald," in former years, some articles by the Pastor. He also wrote a booklet on the first Book of Timothy, called " The Good Minister of Jesus Christ," which many read, valued and esteemed.

Of Pastor W. J. Williams, Pastor H. Dawson writes : " I have very happy recollections of the ministry of Pastor W. J. Williams when he came as a minister to Bradford. He commenced a Bible Class and gave us Bible Readings. I can really say that these studies whetted my appetite for the Bible more than any other ministry I had heard up to that time."

PASTORAL WORK

Although the two brothers journeyed far, both in Britain

and abroad, in addition they also each had the care of a church, or churches, in the British Isles. For some years, as we have noted, Pastor D. P. Williams was located in a pastorate at Pontypridd, and he also ministered at Skewen, near Neath, but for most of his years of ministry he was stationed at Penygroes, General Headquarters of the Apostolic Church. He was President of the Apostolic Church Council for twenty-five years, and as such had charge of the head-quarters assembly at Penygroes. Pastor W. J. Williams was also stationed at Penygroes, but later went to Bradford, Llandybie, Cardiff, and finally, from 1943 to 1945, he ministered in Edgware, London.

Despite the burden of his many duties, Pastor D. P. Williams found time to shepherd the districts over which he was Pastor. He was in Pontypridd for a few years from 1921 onwards, and this proved of immense value to the Apostolic Church in the Rhondda Valley. First of all, an Apostolic Church was established at Pontypridd. This was in fulfilment of a prophecy that had been given previously : " If you are faithful, I will establish a Church at Pontypridd." In this town the Pastor had splendid support from elders David Jones and Percy Johns. The latter, a schoolmaster, was well known as the son of " Periander," a famous Ponty-pridd minister.

This is the testimony of those two elders : " Pastor D. P. Williams came to Pontypridd when the Church was in the balance. Many were deeply wounded, and others very dis-appointed at the condition of the assembly. Many thought the good work begun in the town would collapse. But soon the members were thoroughly convinced that a man of God had settled among them. He proved himself to be a good shepherd, and soon won the confidence of the assembly."

Daniel excelled himself in keeping men together. His ability, helped by God, to heal breaches and unite the saints in the bonds of peace, was amazing. Many testified to his sterling qualities as a minister of Christ. They esteemed him highly, because of the comfort and help they received through his ministry. They felt God had sent them one who had the love of a father and the wisdom of a teacher.

The two elders went on to say : " The crisis was over, the Church found its balance, the life of the members changed as well as the nature of the meetings, the tone of which was now heavenly, and the fellowship sweet. God was not only using His servant to build and establish the church, but also to gather in new members. Baptismal services were frequently held, thirty-seven people being immersed at one service. Many Christians were also baptized with the Holy Spirit."

Several Pentecostal assemblies in the district soon joined the Apostolic Church. In 1920, Pastors D. P. Williams and J. O. Jones visited the Blaenrhondda Assembly, which was the first in the Rhondda to open its doors to the Apostolic vision. In 1921 Bethlehem, Clydach Vale Assembly and Blaenclydach came into the fellowship, and soon Cwmparc, at the head of the valley, followed this example.

A processional march, headed by a band, with hundreds of Apostolic members behind it, passed along the eight miles of the valley. At the head, on horseback, rode Pastors D. P. Williams, Thomas Jones and T. Rees. So many people singing the songs of Zion had a great influence on the Rhondda people. Soon Trealaw, Tonypandy, Blaencwm, Tonyrefail, Porth, Trebanog, Pontygwaith, Abertridwr and Maerdy became enthusiastic for the divine order to be established in their assemblies. The work in the Rhondda, in fact, prospered exceedingly, rich testimony to the sound pastoral work accomplished by Pastor D. P. Williams in Pontypridd assembly and in the Rhondda.

During the four and a half years Pastor D. P. Williams

sojourned in Skewen district the church was filled with great power, and his ministry proved of great benefit to the members. Previously Pastor J. J. Williams had been used to establish the work, and under his ministry many young men were brought into the church, several of whom are now themselves in the ministry.

And so the good work went on under the ministry of Pastor D. P. Williams. One night, while he and some helpers were holding a Cottage Meeting at Resolven, some of the young men present were so overwhelmed by the power of God that they fell prostrate on the floor. The divine visitation at a Skewen Christmas Convention was also so remarkable that some Pentecostal brethren, visiting there, resolved at once to join the Apostolic Church.

While stationed in Penygroes, the Pastor continued to shepherd the flock in his own inimitable way, with firmness and kindness, following the pattern of the Good Shepherd. Everyone who sat under his ministry and pastorate testified to this fact. During his sojourn in that part of Wales, the work made substantial progress.

The same can be said of the ministry of his brother, Pastor W. J. Williams. At the time of his Homecall, which took place in London in 1945, the Cardiff Assembly, of which he had been in charge for a number of years, sent word that a wreath should be bought on their behalf, bearing a card inscribed : " In cherished and loving memory of a great little shepherd."

He lived in Cardiff and London when these cities were being blitzed. During those dark days he showed more concern for the church members than he did for himself. In both cities he went to immense trouble to ensure that his flock were cared for and nursed. The overseer of the Cardiff Assembly, brother F. Atkins, has recorded : " After every enemy raid Pastor Williams went out visiting the members, ministering to their needs. The members could not speak too highly of him, and those bombed out of their houses especially thanked God for his devotion to his work and his kindness to them. He did this in spite of the fact that his own home was partly demolished in one raid. In his own physical weakness, he went to see the flock to inquire how they were after the raids."

Prophetical ministry came one night at Cardiff, when those present were told that " No harm would befall the members in the House of God." During the heaviest blitz the city suffered this was fulfilled. The people in the houses near the church ran to it and found safety. The vestry had a galvanised roof, and the shrapnel rebounded over it, but not a soul was hurt. In spite of the blackout, the evening meetings were well attended. During Special Meetings the Pastor called on members with a car and took them to the church.

Pastor W. J. Williams was also held in high esteem in other Districts where he resided, including the Yorkshire section of the Church. Pastor H. Dawson, a former President of the Apostolic Church, wrote : " I was greatly blessed to see his aptitude and enthusiasm for pastoral work. The assembly in Great Horton, Bradford, flourished under his care."

The strains and burdens of these servants of God were greatly lightened by the comfort and wise counsel of their wives. Pastor W. J. Williams's first wife was Mary Ann Evans, whom he married at Llandeilo on January 25, 1912. They had three children, the present Mrs. John Evans, wife of an Apostolic Church Pastor in Dublin, and Mark, who married Lois, daughter of the late Pastor W. H. Lewis, London. One of the three children died in infancy. How much Mrs. Williams sacrificed can be gathered from the fact that he spent only one Christmas at home during his public ministry.

The brothers Williams went to Australia in September, 1934. At the time, Mrs. W. J. Williams was very ill, and the doctor warned that there was no hope of recovery. The mother showed great faith and fortitude. She told her husband : " You must go, the Lord has called you to go. I have never said ' No ' to His will during all the years, and I will not say it now, before He takes me home. If He takes me while you are away, all will be well."

Pastor W. J. Williams was guided through prophetical ministry to go to Australia, being assured that " the Lord would look after his handmaid while he was away." And Mrs. Williams was alive to welcome her husband on his return. Much to the sorrow of all who knew her, her home call came on November 15, 1936, when she was forty-nine years of age.

In 1938 Pastor W. J. Williams married again, his second wife being the daughter of the much esteemed John and Rachel Evans, of Capel Isaac, Llandeilo. She was a widow and had one son, David Omri. She proved a source of great help and inspiration to her husband, especially during the blitz. They had one child, Ruth.

ADMINISTRATION

Because of the rapid growth of the Church in the early years, the two brothers were bound to undertake a great deal of administrative work. In the process of the years a fuller complement of apostles and prophets gathered in Councils to direct the affairs of the Church. But in the beginning when major difficulties arose from time to time in any assembly or district, the two Pastors had to make visits to restore order and unity. When Pentecostal assemblies

wished to join the Apostolic Church, the brothers had
to explain the Apostolic tenets to them.

They had to decide from time to time with others which
towns and villages were to have pioneering campaigns, and
which places were to have new assemblies. Ministry also
had to be provided for the ever-growing number of churches,
on week nights as well as Sundays. This was arranged
through a Monthly Ministry Plan, and speakers had to be
chosen and prepared for these appointments.

District and Local Elders' Meetings were held and attended
by the Pastors, to discuss all aspects of Church work. Added
to this administrative work was the exacting business of the
four Missionary Councils each year, in addition to Executive
meetings in between. In these meetings, Pastor D. P. Williams
was Chairman. Grave problems had to be faced and settled.
Consideration had to be given to the calling-out of full-time
ministers for the Home field, and the sending of missionaries
to foreign fields. When changes of ministers were desirable
it had to be decided which ministers were to move to new
districts.

Duties and obligations kept increasing, and it is no wonder
that physical prostration was the experience of Pastor D. P.
Williams. Yet he laboured on and conquered. Also Pastor
W. J. Williams, without complaint, faithfully did his part as
a prophet in the upbuilding of the Church.

CHAPTER TEN

OUTSTANDING CHARACTERISTICS

ALTHOUGH Pastors D. P. and W. J. Williams were brothers in the flesh, there were considerable differences in personality between them. Physically Pastor D. P. Williams was much taller than his brother, who was small in stature. They were also dissimilar in other ways, and in this chapter we shall mention some of them.

Those who heard Pastor D. P. Williams preach will never forget the impression produced by his striking personality and by the dramatic manner he had of presenting his message. The spare figure, the noble head, flung back in moments of inspiration, the sleek black hair, the piercing eyes, the mobile lips, the strong, well modulated voice—all combined to produce the impression of a preacher of rare distinction. The effect of all this on the congregation was on occasion overwhelming, dealing as he did with the deep things of God, yet never in a ponderous or obscure manner. Always he held the attention and interest of his congregation, and at times they experienced a sense of exhilaration such as rarely comes to those who occupy the pew. He had, as has already been stated, remarkable eyes. They were very dark brown in colour, bright and piercing, and they dominated an audience, and reflected the purity and nobility of the man who possessed them.

His brother, though outstanding as a prophet, was also a notable preacher. Lacking perhaps the depth of his brother, he was, nevertheless, if anything, rather more forceful. He had a combative manner which found expression in his preaching. His voice was not so strong as that of Daniel, nor was his appearance so striking, but he possessed under

God the power to sway large congregations. Often he produced a profoundly moving effect upon his hearers. His sermons were sometimes interrupted by the jubilant exclamations of the congregation.

As a writer he was in some ways superior to his brother, although not as productive. He had an eye for interesting situations, a masterly grasp of facts and a lucidity of expression that was very telling.

As we have seen, Pastor D. P. Williams travelled extensively, leaving behind him a favourable impression wherever he went. He had a pleasing personality, and was a man of great gentleness and kindness. His sufferings as a youth, no doubt, had made him considerate of others and sensitive to every kind of anguish wherever he came upon it. Determined in the face of difficulties, he had great courage and strength of will. Yet he was also loving and sympathetic. People always felt better after being in his company.

One Sunday he visited Belle Vue Chapel, Swansea. There he met a confirmed criminal who had been in prison thirty-two times. Only that morning he had arrived in Swansea after walking from Gloucester Prison. In these services he came forward in deep prostration, seeking Christ. One morning it was arranged for Pastor D. P. Williams to meet him, but the Pastor missed him, and the man came to Penygroes and met the Pastor at a prayer meeting. A bed was improvized for the converted crook in the hall. He was washed, clothed and fed, and work was found for him. The assembly befriended him, and he was given every chance to achieve a new life.

Being upset at work over something or other, he left his employment and went away. Later, however, he wrote and apologised to the Pastor. Everybody said he was a dangerous man, and should not be encouraged to return, but Pastor D. P. Williams realized that the man had a soul to save, so on his return he admitted him to his help and friendship once more.

The Pastor's gentleness and kindness enabled him to handle difficult situations with great tact and wisdom. His Pastorate in Skewen did not commence as he had expected. The members of that District were delighted at the prospect of having a Pastor who was the President of the Church Council. Yet for some reason he did not feel settled in the new Pastorate. Possibly it may have arisen from the fact that he was away ministering more often than the previous Pastor and therefore not able to give as much personal attention to the members.

Nevertheless, he applied himself unceasingly to prayer. For weeks, day and night, he pleaded with God to help him. Digging in the large garden at the rear of the house, on one occasion, he unearthed a piece of the root of a tree. It was as hard as flint and in the form of a perfect cross. This caused him to think of Calvary, and he leaned upon his spade in silent worship. In those moments he heard the still small voice instructing him regarding his ministry, and he determined that, henceforth, the Cross should be his theme to the people of Skewen.

Night after night, for months on end, there flowed from his full heart and fluent tongue a teaching ministry from the Roman Epistle such as will never be forgotten by those who were privileged to hear it. The atmosphere of the church changed, as one after another received the word of truth, transforming their life and character. He hung the cross found in the garden above his desk, where it became perfectly white and which to this day is in the possession of his widow.

In his early married life he was somewhat ambitious and longed to own a large house. In the house he did then occupy a room at the front was reserved for the fine new furniture he planned to have and money was set aside systematically towards its purchase.

This was the situation when a gipsy knocked at his door. The gipsy was filled with demonic power, but the Pastor charged the evil spirits to depart in the Name of Jesus; and, with a loud yell, they did, leaving the poor man as if dead. Later he became serene and peaceful, and invited the Pastor to his tent in a field some distance away.

The following night, undeterred by the wintry conditions, several believers went through boggy fields to the tent in which the gipsy lived. There were sacks on the ground, an old boiler, a bed of straw and a box which contained all they possessed. The Pastor went in and read the Word of God, and soon the gipsy's wife was earnestly seeking salvation.

For the man the Pastor found work at a local colliery, and for some weeks, efforts were made to obtain more suitable accommodation for them, but without success. Then the Lord told Pastor D. P. Williams in his heart that if he really loved the gipsies, he would open his front room to them. At first, the Pastor resisted the command, but finally he knelt and pledged that he would give up the precious room.

His wife protested that such an action would break her heart, but when he explained all that had happened, she readily agreed to give up the room, and next night the gipsies took possession. For the first time those poor people had chairs to sit on and a bed to sleep in. They were washed, clothed and fed. But the experiences that followed were far from agreeable, as the gipsies did not find it easy to change their former habits. Pastor D. P. Williams said to the Lord: " It is too much. We cannot bear it any longer." Soon afterwards, the gipsies left the home. Never again had the Pastor a desire for a grand home.

In after life he proved very humble in his actions and in his church life. Travelling as he did to many countries, he never lost his sense of humility, remaining true to the Pauline injunction to ' be all things to all men.' His belief was that lordliness in any Christian believer, especially in God's servants, was a gross misrepresentation of the self-denying spirit of Christ. The Pastor had an unassuming manner and a deep humility of heart and transparent sincerity, that disarmed all suspicion or fear, and made it easy to open one's heart for fellowship with him, and have counsel and help from him. In business meetings he was never officious and overbearing as a chairman, but very humble.

He had also a forgiving spirit. It is a quality he needed greatly, especially in the early years of his ministry. Where ever he went he encountered lies concerning the Apostolic Church. He found minds prejudiced against him, but he never retaliated or so much as tried to defend himself, believing that truth would survive all efforts to pervert it.

On one occasion he received a series of letters charged with malice and hatred, though he had done nothing to deserve them. When he showed one of these letters to a close friend and was asked what he meant to do about it, he simply placed the missive in the fire. " That's what we'll do," he said. " Now, let us pray for the poor fellow."

Our first President had, also, a personal disinterestedness in finance. While in Denmark, he was asked if he had used his position to collect money for himself and for the leaders of the Apostolic Church. Evangelist W. T. Evans was present, and he gave this independent, impartial opinion regarding the matter. " After being led to join the Apostolic Church, I was informed by a certain person that the brethren in the church were obtaining money from people, and that they owned many rows of houses. I investigated this story for myself and found it to be false. I have known Pastor

Williams for a number of years, and I know he has no riches in this world. It is rather, perhaps, intimate to say, but he will forgive it, I am sure, that I have seen him bringing home small pieces of leather to mend his children's shoes. That does not speak of much wealth. I have known him many times without money to pay his train fare. Another brother made another accusation. I investigated that also, and I found it to be false. I can vouch, as a servant of God today that there is no self-interest in the brethren of the Apostolic Church, or I should immediately have left it. Pastor Williams's concern was not for cash, but for conversions and consecrations."

Again, his faith in God remained unshaken even under the severest trial. Once it happened that his two younger children fell dangerously ill. Day and night the whole house was in a state of watchful anxiety. At the same time Pastor Williams suffered a severe attack of pneumonia. While he was in this condition his wife asked him to pray for the recovery of the children, as they were so seriously ill. The Devil immediately whispered to him : " Why pray for them when you have no faith for yourself ?" But, believing the promises in the Word of God, he prayed for his children and anointed them. Next morning both asked for something to eat, and from that moment they, and the father, began to recover.

An outstanding incident revealing the appreciation of the Pastor by others, even outside of the Apostolic fellowship. occurred during a memorial service on board ship, when he and his wife were outward bound for North America. I was made known that President Roosevelt had died, and the Pastor was asked to conduct a memorial service in remembrance of the American President. This was attended by the ship's company, and a large congregation of passengers

Much blessing ensued, and many were the tears shed during the service.

Pastor W. J. Williams had also many outstanding characteristics. He fought for the honour of the Apostolic Church, and for its comprehensive truth. He was a man of immense courage in his stand for the basic principles of the Gospel. Small of stature, he was nevertheless a giant in determination. So much so that physical weakness could not prevent him carrying out his duties. In extreme instances, illnesses laid him low, but the moment his strength returned, he was again about his Master's business. Yet he knew how hopeless it was to attempt any task, save in the power of Holy Spirit, his mainstay in all his manifold undertakings.

He travelled in many countries, preaching the full Gospel, and was a faithful preacher and minister of the Word. His perseverance was of that high order which made it possible for him to press on dauntlessly to the end. He once said that he had tried to keep a vow made to his father, "that he would never say he could not do a thing until he had failed in the attempt."

Again, he had an unreserved love for Christ and for the cause of Christ. Pastor T. V. Lewis remarked at his memorial service : "He was a burning light, burning in activity and fervency. He was also a shining light. He shone before others by his life and testimony."

He had a great love for the children of God, and always responded at once to the call of neighbours in distress, his motor car being at the disposal of any urgent case. He lived unselfishly, and was ever ready to share the cares and burdens of others, never sparing himself in his efforts to impart a blessing, and following faithfully the example of his Master by going about doing good.

"He told me once," wrote Pastor Thomas Davies, "of the crises he was in when diphtheria broke out in the district,

and of his agony of mind on hearing of the deaths of infants
in the neighbourhood. His own daughter (May) had contracted the dread disease and was at the point of death.
He felt led by God to ask the doctor in attendance to take
any risks attendant on an operation. Tracheotomy was the
only means of cure, and the doctors operated on the child,
and it proved successful."

Finally, courage was needed, for he had often to give forth
the prophetic ministry in the face of opposition. Pastor W. J.
Williams suffered as a prophet, and was willing to do so.
Being called as a prophet, he knew he had a path of suffering
before him. He said not long before he died : " If I had
known beforehand what I had to face as a prophet, the
persecution, slights and suffering I have met and endured
during the last twenty years and more, I would never have
commenced the journey." He added : " But His grace has
been sufficient, and He has never failed me."

Pastor D. P. Williams in Estonia and Latvia
in 1935

Sacred to the Memory Of

DANIEL
POWELL WILLIAMS
BELOVED HUSBAND OF
MABEL WILLIAMS,
CLANYRAFON, CORSLAS,
DIED 13TH FEB. 1947,
AGED 64 YEARS.

ERECTED TO A BELOVED
PRESIDENT AS A TOKEN OF
LOVE AND ESTEEM BY THE
OFFICERS AND MEMBERS
OF THE
APOSTOLIC CHURCH
IN THE BRITISH ISLES
AND OVERSEAS.

Grave of the late Pastor D. P. Williams

CHAPTER ELEVEN

APOSTLE–PROPHET MINISTRY

IF any man of the twentieth century was an Apostle, our first President was. The ministers and members of the Church recognized his quality and status as such. There is no doubt that he had the spiritual credentials and qualifications necessary for this office. He was, as we have noted, the first Apostle to be ordained in the Apostolic Church.

As an Apostle, he was responsible for the spiritual status and condition of his brother, the prophet, and for his development. It is the work of all apostles to assist in this way in the maturing of prophets. He helped his brother by encouraging him in the Lord, and by an appreciation of the true prophetical ministry that came through him. Understanding the prophets and their difficulties, and also the true nature of prophecy, he was able to help them.

The commission of the pastor as an apostle was general and not limited to any section of the Church. His vision was large, reaching out to many nations and peoples. He strove to spread the full Gospel everywhere, afterwards seeking to nourish and cherish the converts. Thus he became the father and founder of many churches.

A valuable guide and guardian of the Church with regard to doctrine, he helped to interpret it to the Church, announcing no new dogmas, but proclaiming eternal truths from the Holy Scriptures that never change. He helped to make the members of the Church Christlike, and also to cleanse, purify and sanctify them. Many felt the cleansing power of the Written Word as it flowed from him to them.

When necessary, he also undertook to discipline the members of the Church, but only with the longsuffering mentioned by the Apostle Paul. Never did he expel members from the fellowship except when no other course was possible. Pastor B. J. Noot writes : " Pastor D. P. Williams once said to me, ' Whatever the condition of any backslider, however far they may have gone astray and however difficult they may prove to be, never give them up '."

An as apostle he had authority to lay hands on the converts that they might receive the baptism of the Holy Spirit (Acts 8), and on certain Church members that they might receive spiritual gifts (Rom. 1 : 11). He also had power to ordain certain brethren into office, among them overseers, elders and evangelists, according to the qualifications laid down in the Scriptures (I Tim. 3).

He also received revelation of other apostles, prophets and full-time ministers in the church. Pastor B. J. Noot relates : " As a young man I was an elder in Skewen Church. One day, coming from the Sunday School, we were crossing a bridge together, when Pastor D. P. Williams suddenly stopped and put his arm around me. I thought it strange, and felt embarrassed, as many were passing at the time. Yet I forgot the incident until seven years later, when I was called into the apostleship. I was leaving Cardiff for another pastorate at the time, and the Pastor came from Penygroes to the farewell service. When he spoke he said : ' I am sure that Pastor Noot will remember this incident. Years ago, when he was a young man, we were crossing the bridge at Skewen, when the Lord said to me : ' Put your arm around this young man, I want you to cherish him, he is my apostle '.' Several years later I was called to that office."

Many revelations were given by prophetical ministry, through his brother and others, but as more apostles were called the apostleship carried much of the weight of administration in the Church, while the prophets continued to contribute greatly to the benefit of the Councils and

Executives by giving many precious words of the Lord. Pastor D. P. Williams was a man who ever sought the face of God for divine revelation, and conveyed it to the church in his apostleship.

The signs of an apostle were revealed in Pastor D. P. Williams's life by power, prayer and preaching. He had the power to perform signs and wonders in the Name of Jesus Christ. This book proves this, although it was by no means his chief ministry. A man of prayer above all, he lived in prayer, spending hours a day in prayer for the sake of the work, giving much time also to the study of the Word of God, and preaching it with great liberty and acceptance. Another evidence of his apostleship was that under his ministry many people were saved and baptized with the Holy Spirit, and churches were also established by him (I Cor. 9 : 1, 2).

The plan of God is that apostles and prophets should work together and in co-operation maintain a close spiritual fellowship. They will thus have a deeper understanding of the will of God for His Church. In the many years during which the two Pastors worked together as apostle and prophet, God greatly blessed their ministry. When at home in the British Isles they often went around the assemblies together, with apostolic and prophetical ministry. On occasions the apostle would minister from the Scripture, and on other occasions prophetical ministry would be given, the apostle expounding and applying it with great impressiveness.

The following will indicate how God was at that time revealing Himself to Pastor W. J. Williams. This experience occurred while the two brothers were in Copenhagen, Denmark, in 1924. Pastor W. J. Williams one night had a dream. Next morning at the breakfast table he described it. He said that he saw Pastors D. P. Williams, H. Cousen and T. Davies in a room together, a room with two doors.

Pastor Hollis, our first missionary in the Apostolic Church, came through one of the doors, and placed on the table a cable on which was the word 'never,' and then went out through the same door. The other door opened and a young couple came in and knelt down. Pastors D. P. Williams and H. Cousen laid hands upon them, then the two went out through the same door by which Pastor Hollis had left. No more was said, but as time went on unfortunately certain events happened that proved the dream to be all too true, and given of God, for Pastor Hollis soon resigned from the Missionary Staff, and the young man seen in the dream was given his place as Superintendent of the field, his young wife going with him to the Argentine.

Through the prophetical ministry of Pastor W. J. Williams and other channels lasting and notable benefits have been brought to the Church. One of the benefits is a wonderful unity within its borders. The prophetic office was one of the most decisive means of bringing the sections of the Church in the British Isles into one. The prophetic office proved to be one in the essence of truth and revelation and so made the members one in every respect.

The prophetic word also came through Pastor W. J. Williams sending apostles and prophets to proclaim the Gospel in far-off lands, and as a result great things were accomplished. Through him the prophetic word came that certain servants were to go to Australia, Nigeria, America, New Zealand and other countries. A great movement has come into being in the British Isles and in other nations through the spoken word that came so faithfully through him and others. The Apostolic Temple at Penygroes and the Apostolic Church Bible College owe their existence to prophetic utterances through Pastor W. J. Williams.

In the early years of the church's life—that is, in the 1920's —enlightenment was sought and given regarding personal matters to the servants of God. Today the major burdens undertaken by the prophets have to do with church and spiritual matters, but it will be profitable to record one or two events which took place in past days, which were a source of much encouragement, and caused God's people to believe that God was indeed speaking in our day and generation.

Pastor T. V. Lewis relates how, while working in Clydach Vale and attending Bethlehem Church there, he joined the Apostolic fellowship. A prophetical word came through Pastor W. J. Williams and advised him to leave his work at the Cambrian Colliery and seek work at the Ocean Colliery, Cwmparc, at the head of the Rhondda Valley. The counsel given was : " Take the first employment that is offered, and I will help you, for I want you to take charge of the assemblies at Cwmparc and Blaenrhondda."

This created a problem for him, as he was earning good money at Clydach Vale. Yet, obeying the instruction, he applied for work at Cwmparc, only to be told by the manager that no work was available. At that moment a man happened to be coming from the pit and must have heard what had been said. He spoke to the manager, who then said to Pastor Lewis : " You can have employment by working at the coal face." Pastor Lewis, however, was a haulier, yet he decided to accept the offer.

At the Cambrian Colliery they had electric lamps, but at Cwmparc they had only oil lamps. The man in charge told him that the only place to which he could send him was so terrible it was called "The Dardanelles." In fact, a man who had started only that morning, had looked at it and left. Despite this discouragement, and because he believed that God had spoken to him, he went to the stall and prayed : " Lord, teach me to be a collier. I am here on Thy Word."

The place was in a very bad condition, and not long after he had begun work, a pit prop collapsed and with it came down a great deal of rubbish. When he had cleared the rubbish away, he saw that it had exposed a splendid face of coal, one as smooth as a rock. He had never before seen such a fine face of coal, and soon he was filling trams with the precious mineral. Workmen came from all over the pit to see the remarkable change in the coal face. More remarkably, the Cambrian Colliery closed down six months later and was idle for five years, while Pastor T. V. Lewis worked continually in the pit to which the Lord prophetically had directed him.

Pastor T. Davies was plagued with chronic appendicitis from 1924 to 1928. The pain became unbearable, and one Sunday at midnight, being in agony he went seeking God's guidance. A prophetic word came through Pastor W. J. Williams, saying: " I will tell thee something incredible. Thou needest not go to the hospital. Take a glassful of the fruit of the lemon tree with water and My servant will call to see thee towards evening." When asked if he believed the word, he replied, " Of course, I am going to act on it !"

Reaching home, he asked his wife to make him a jugful of lemon essence and water. Lying in bed, he kept sipping the liquid, and felt a release of his appendix. The pain increased as the lemon essence and water made their way through the stomach and intestines, and finally he ejected a greyish sausage-shaped mass. The pain never troubled him again. In the Apostolic Church today we do not make enquiries regarding divine healing, recognizing that the proper course prescribed in the Scriptures is as follows : " Is any sick among you, let them call for the elders," not the prophet. Nevertheless, it is remarkable how God answered the Apostolic members in their simplicity of faith in the early days of the work.

There were also many predictive words that came through Pastor W. J. Williams, words that were literally fulfilled. The

Scriptures state that one of the ways by which God's people can know whether God has spoken through the prophet is, whether the word comes to pass or not. If it is fulfilled, then it is the Word of the Lord ; if not, then it is not His Word.

As stated already, the word of prophecy foretold in a Penygroes Convention in 1919, before the Apostolic Church had sent forth any missionaries, that God was going to bring thither from afar people of coloured races, and this has been wonderfully fulfilled. Pastor W. J. Williams was also used as a prophet to foretell that bombs would be dropped on London in World War I. This, too, came to pass. While in Belfast, in 1920, prophetical ministry also came through the Pastor foretelling that blood would run in the streets of that city in the near future. This came to pass as predicted.

During the World War II, when our leaders had grave problems to face, prophetical ministry came in a church executive in June 1940, that because of God's plan Britain would be victorious, not that we should be exalted as a nation, but because of His purpose. The last war was one of the greatest crises through which Great Britain ever passed, and which could have brought unspeakable disaster to her as a nation. One after another the countries of Europe fell, while Britain stood alone against the might of Germany. She would no doubt have fallen but for the intervention of God, intervention that took place on many occasions and in many ways.

This extremely anxious period in the summer of 1940 did not prevent the members of the General Executive from meeting at the prescribed times. They met at Wem, Shropshire, during June, and in one of the sessions a special prophetical word was given through Pastor W. J. Williams, which was as follows : " There is a spiritual kingdom that will function eternally in the ages to come. But there is a natural kingdom, and if you would like a definite word regarding the war that is going on, as for victory, I will give victory to your country. Now where is faith to believe, and where is the test of the prophetical ministry, regarding the future in the most difficult time in history ? Disaster impending, blackness gathering, clouds hovering, the nations trembling and thrones quivering. I am declaring now in your midst, few as you are, as for victory, victory will come, but not because of virtue or merit. Nay, verily, but I am telling you that, according to My movements in the unseen realm, from country to country, I am moving, brooding, destroying those things that are in the way, so that I may establish the Kingdom that must come even earthwards."

It may, to some who read this book, seem unscriptural to claim that there are apostles and prophets in the church today, but the Scriptures in Ephesians 4 : 11-13 clearly state that these offices were given till we all come into the unity of the faith, and members of the Church as a whole are certainly not there as yet. There is a distinct difference between the apostles of the Lamb, and the ascension apostles of Ephesians 4 : 11. The apostles of the Lamb were given by Christ while he sojourned on earth, but these other apostles were imparted after Christ had ascended on high. (See Ephesians 4 : 7-11). There are twelve apostles of the Lamb and there is no succession from them or addition to them. On the other hand, there are at least ten other apostles mentioned in the Scriptures who were given after Christ ascended on high. Our Lord will continue to give them in every century until He comes for His complete and fully-united Church.

PART VI

DESPATCHES FROM THE FRONT

CHAPTER TWELVE

PULPIT ECHOES

AS we have earlier observed, there are many editorials and sermons of Pastor D. P. Williams in past issues of the "Riches of Grace" and the "Apostolic Herald," and in addition he has published several booklets. Yet there are quite a number of his sermons and Bible Readings still unpublished. Pastor W. J. Williams had a number of his sermons published in the church magazines, and he also left many unpublished. In this chapter we print some outlines of their sermons, and excerpts from them.

First, those of Pastor D. P. Williams.

LEAVEN

1. The Leaven of 'Justification by Works.'
2. The Leaven of 'Sanctification by Self-mortification.'
3. The Leaven of 'The Doctrine of a larger Hope.'
4. The Leaven of 'Prayers for the Dead.'
5. The Leaven of 'Jesus, an Ideal Man.'

————

THE CHURCH (Matt. 16 : 13-19)

1. Revelation : 'Flesh and blood has not revealed this unto thee.'
2. Confession : 'Thou art the Christ, the Son of the Living God.'
3. Election : 'I will give' v. 19.
4. Separation : 'Church' translates 'Ecclesia,' which means the 'Called Out.'

THE LORD'S TABLE (I Cor. 11 : 23, 24)

1. Deportment :
   - (a) Modesty at the Lord's Table.
   - (b) Manners of saints at the Lord's Table.
   - (c) Meaning of the Lord's Table.

2. Principles :
   - (a) Commemoration. This do in Remembrance.
     - i. With wonder.
     - ii. With reverence.
     - iii. With delight.
     - iv. With gratitude.
   - (b) Declaration. ' For as often as ye eat.'
   - (c) Separation. ' The Lord's Table divides.'
   - (d) Examination. ' Let a man examine himself.'
   - (e) Consideration. ' Tarry one for another.'
   - (f) Participation. ' Eat and drink.'

REVELATION 13

1. The Beast.
2. The Beast's Image.
3. The Mark of the Beast.
4. The Number of the Beast.

SUFFERING (II Tim. 2 : 12)

1. The Exhortation to Suffering.
2. The Suffering of our Lord.
3. Suffering and the Risen Life.
4. The Challenge of Suffering.
5. The Fellowship of His Sufferings.
6. Sufferings and the Body of Christ.
7. Sufferings and the Reigning Life.

EBENEZER

" Hitherto hath the Lord helped us " (I Sam. 7 : 12)

1. Israel : Their Condition.
2. Israel : Their Contrition.
3. Israel : Their Consecration.

THE DIACONATE (Acts 6)

1. The Manner in which deacons were introduced.
2. The Duties they were expected to exercise.
3. The Qualifications which were demanded of them.
   - (a) Honesty or Integrity.
   - (b) Wisdom or Sagacity.
   - (c) Spirituality or Fulness of the Holy Spirit.

THE GODHEAD (Gen. 1 : 1)

1. The Being of God.
2. The Nature of God.
   - (a) God is Love.   (b) God is Spirit.
3. The Attributes of God.
   - (a) Omnipotence.   (b) Omniscience.   (c) Omnipresence.

BEHOLD, THE LAMB OF GOD (John 1 : 29)

1. Substitution : ' Behold the Lamb.'
2. Superiority : ' Preferred before Me.'
3. Priority : ' He was before Me.'
4. Manifestation : ' That He should be made manifest to Israel.'
5. Authentication : ' The Spirit descending.'
6. Administrations : ' He shall baptise with the Holy Spirit.'
7. Attestation : ' I saw and bear witness that this was the Son of God.'

PAUL, THE MODEL MAN

" I was not disobedient to the heavenly Vision " (Acts 26 : 19)

1. Paul a pattern in his Conversion (Acts 9 : 3).
2. Paul a pattern in his Consecration (Acts 9 : 6).
3. Paul a pattern in his Commission (Acts 9 : 15).
4. Paul a pattern in his Declaration (Acts 26 : 19).

SECOND ADVENT (I Thess.)

1. The Second Coming in relation to the Ministry (2 : 19).
2. The Second Coming in relation to Church Unity (3 : 12, 13).
```
```

3. The Second Coming in relation to the dead (4 : 1-18).
4. The Second Coming in relation to Sanctification (5 : 23-28).

SANCTIFICATION (I Thess. 5 : 23-28)

1. The Author of Sanctification—God.
2. The Nature of Sanctification—Peace.
3. The Extensiveness of Sanctification—Threefold nature of man.
4. The Possibility of Sanctification—Faithfulness.
5. The Longing for Sanctification—Pray for us.
6. The Expression of Sanctification—Holy Kiss.

MATTHEW 16

1. The Revelation of Christ (Matt. 16 : 16).
2. The Revelation of the Church (Matt. 16 : 18).
3. The Revelation of the Cross (Matt. 16 : 21-24).
4. The Revelation of His Coming (Matt. 16 : 27).

THE ETERNAL KING (John 19 : 14)

1. The Intimated King (Gen. 3 : 15).
2. The Covenanted King (II Sam. 7 : 8-12).
3. The Appointed King (Psalm 2 : 6).
4. The Appeared King (Matt. 2 : 1-3).
5. The Presented King (Matt. 3 : 3).
6. The Rejected King (John 1 : 11).
7. The Exalted King (Heb. 1 : 3).
8. The Returning King (Acts 1 : 11).
9. The Reigning King (Psalm 2 : 9).

TRINITY

The word " Trinity " was first used in theology in a treatise for its defence by Theophilus, Bishop of Antioch in Syria, between the years 168 and 183 A.D. It is derived from the Latin ' Trinitas,' which means ' three-fold,' ' Three in One,' and in that sense it has been used to convey the Divine

mystery of the Three Persons in Unity in the Godhead. (See
" Systematic Theology " by Prof. Hodge). We cannot deal
with the Unity of the Godhead independently of its threefold
nature inasmuch as the Divine Essence has manifested itself
in Three Persons, Father, Son and Holy Spirit. We observe
in the Holy Scriptures the plurality of names recorded for
the One God. God speaks of Himself in plural pronouns,
as in, " Let us make man in Our Own Image, and after Our
Own Likeness," and, " And the Lord God said, behold the
man is become as one of Us, to know good and evil," and
" Let Us go down " (Gen. 1 : 26 ; 3 : 22 ; 11 : 1).

THE BAPTISMAL FORMULA (Matt. 28 : 19)

The original formula of our Lord's commission to His
disciples was given in the full comprehensive Name—Creator,
Redeemer, Comforter. It states, "baptizing them in the Name
of the Father, and of the Son, and of the Holy Spirit," the
Three Persons being mentioned distinctly and separately, over
which there is no ground of controversy. It is true that we
find the Name " Jesus " only mentioned in the Acts of the
Apostles as a form of expression when they were baptizing.
Yet the Apostles' Creed, as we read the substance of it in
the various Epistles, involves the acknowledgement of the
whole Godhead. The disciples baptized in the Name of Jesus
in order to emphasize the important truth that was to be
established especially in the hearts of the Jews, that Jesus
of Nazareth, whom they had despised and rejected, was the
very God Jehovah, Who had become incarnate for our
salvation. But it is best to adhere to the general tone of
the Scripture, which gives undeniable proof that there are
Three Persons in the Unity of the Godhead, and to adhere
to the original formula.

ONE GOD (Ephes. 4 : 6)

The One God is spoken of in the Scripture in a threefold application.

1. One in source and sovereignty—' Above all.'
2. One in immanence and permutability—' Through all.'
3. One in inherence and universality—' And in you all.'

The Apostle makes this statement to distinguish the Christian doctrines from all other theories, and particularly against four errors.

1. Polytheism, an erroneous theory which contends for and advocates plurality of gods. Counter to this statement we have Paul's : " One God and Father of all."

2. Pantheism, an erroneous theory which would persuade us that the universe is god above all. Counter to this, again, Paul states : " Who is above all."

3. Agnosticism, an erroneous theory which asserts that God cannot dwell within evil matter. Confuting this, again Paul writes : " Through all."

4. Materialism, as erroneous as the above, if not more so, which denies the existence of God, and which the apostle counteracts by saying : " And in you all."

THE OMNIPOTENCE OF GOD

When the poet with his imaginative genius composes his essays out of the letters of the alphabet, or the musician composes his melodious anthem out of the seven musical notes, it is evident that there is a mind full of harmony behind it all, causing the listeners to be thrilled. Thus it is with this vast universe which rolls with such rapidity, yet majestically sublime and glorious in harmony. The universe without and the universe within us, the motions of the heart, arteries, veins, blood and other fluids, the members of the body, the perception of the senses, the actions of the mind, the structure of creation, and the countless planets, the production of vegetable and animal life, their growth, functions, perfections and operations, are they not enough to vindicate the truth of the assertion that behind them there is boundless Intelligence and Power, that brought these worlds into existence and unity ? All things around us bear witness to and evince in detail God's limitless power, His stainless character, His exhaustless goodness, and they are expressions of His greatness in Nature, with its terrible force and irresistible energy. Yet this universe is but a fraction of God's creation, and must be regarded as infinitesimal in comparison with the immense and measureless worlds existing in the Unseen. The rushing wind is, as it were, but His breath ; the thunder, His voice ; the lightning, the flash of His eye ; the dawn, the eyelids of His glory ; the flames of the sunset, the beams of His searching Countenance ; the harmony of the spheres, the expression of His finger-tips on the Organ of Creation ; the light, His robes ; the burning sun, His unbearable holiness ; the earth, His footstool ; the oceans, His immense compassion ; volcanoes and earthquakes, the burning of His anger ; His love, the endless, fathomless, measureless, infinite source of all things.

PRESERVATION FROM EVIL FORCES

The conflict was very great in the churches of Asia, apostasy and false philosophy were beginning to invade the Church. This influence was affecting the constitution of the Body of Christ. Is it not true that the days we are living in have a tremendous influence upon the saints of God ? Only those who live close to Jesus, and in the environment of His Throne and Kingdom, will be preserved from the power of the environment of the age. As the Church of Jesus Christ we need to be preserved from the powers of the air, for the god of this world, Satan, is filling, as it were, the air with poisonous gases. The atmosphere is charged with the suggestions of the Prince of Darkness. And God's people, who know the will of God, only can be preserved in mind and heart, through the Holy Spirit, and then they will not belong to this age, but to the age to come. I pray that heaven will come down with such a renewing of the Spirit of Christ, and with such an anointing and illumination that we shall be conformed to the age to come.

———

"Be not conformed to this world, but be ye transformed"
(Rom. 12 : 2)

Let us remember that we are exerting an influence on and in the world and the world upon us. Both act and react upon one another by words, by reactions, by habits. The vice of the ungodly is restrained, yes, and the virtue of the Christian is checked. Therefore there is a growing need of prayerfulness and watchfulness on our part that we may be kept unspotted from the world. We should ever remember that we are called to shine as lights and to purify as salt. The Lord has intended that we should be centres of purifying, healing and elevating influence in the world. Worldly conformity is our conformation to these customs and habits of life, which are not in accord with the will of God, and detrimental to the principles of consecration and holiness, whether intellectual, physical or social. The worldling may cherish vain thoughts, his imaginative chambers may be full of sensual longings. He may array himself in costly dress and sparkling jewellery. He may indulge in drink and vice and worldly behaviour, unclean habits, impure language, foul animalism, card-playing, betting, smoking, theatre-going,

novel-reading of sensual love-stories. He may go half clad
to the dancing saloons and listen to the sinful jazz of a music
hall. Why should we enlarge ? The world is intoxicated
in its mad pursuit of sensation. The Devil of the twentieth
century is a gay, frivolous monster, and all who choose to
follow him will find themselves wallowing in the mire of
pollution and degradation. All these evil habits have no
harmony with prayer, devotion, spiritual meditation and
heavenly aspirations. So, Christian, " be ye not conformed
to this world, but be ye transformed."

THE NEED OF HEALTHY MEMBERS

Every member of the Body of Christ must keep his own
distinctive character in order to derive the grace according
to the gift, and in order to make his contribution to the other
gifted members. How the Holy Spirit must be grieved by
the low, rude, crude and rudimentary types of Christians that
are continually draining the energy from the members of the
Body of Christ and keeping the Church in discontent and
shame, and a derision to the world. Speaking of the problem
of cancer, Dr. J. Murray of the Imperial Cancer Research
Fund, notes that the individual cells of the various tissues
are not independently self contained units, each going its own
way, but that they are subject to the general controlling
influence, which limits their rate and amount of growth, so
that a fairly uniform proportion is maintained between the
different organs and parts of the body. In cancer, this controlling power and influence is wanting. The problem lies
in the discovery that has been made that the cells in the
cancer area have started in their altered tempo of growth.
They are unaffected by the restrained influences which
normally hold the cells of the rest of the body within
their proper bounds. This throws light on the condition of

unhealthy and impure souls. The pure, holy current from God does not act upon and influence their lives. Hence the reason for the anger, malice, jealousy, backbiting, slandering, evil surmising, and filthy communications that are to be found in carnal Christians. The moral cancer has set in, eating the vitals and germinating all manner of disease. But it need not be so if we allow the grace and love of God to fill our hearts and spirits.

THE HOLY SPIRIT IN THE BODY OF CHRIST

"He shall glorify Me, for He shall receive of Mine,
and shall show it unto you" (John 16 : 12-15)

The Holy Spirit was sent from the Throne of God to exercise the Throne Life in the Body of Christ, and to manifest the Headship and the Lordship of Christ. It is only as the Holy Spirit exercises the Lordship of Christ through the members of the Body that they contribute to the Body the things that really are in Christ. Many things may be said and done, great efforts and schemes may be launched, but ambition, excitement, and high-sounding declarations will take us nowhere. They die fruitless. But the Holy Spirit perpetuating the Heavenly Order is no mechanism, officialism or denominationalism. He is a spiritual force, producing Divine results according to the order and principles of the indwelling life, and in the Church, exhibited by certain gifts and functions which express their position by revealing Christ. Is it not very important that they who are in active service should be full of the Holy Spirit, knowing of the deep work of the Cross in their nature, crucified with Christ, and being fully subject to the Head ? Before they can be the means of nourishing and building up the Body unto perfection it must be so.

MY GOSPEL

The Apostle Paul spoke of five Gospels : (1) The Gospel of Grace ; (2) The Gospel of the Kingdom ; (3) The Gospel of the Throne ; (4) The Gospel of Man ; (5) The Everlasting Gospel. The Gospel of the Throne was Paul's "My Gospel," and also it refers to the new revelation given to Paul, that of the mystical Body of Christ. When Pentecost came there was a change in the plan of God. Salvation was not a new thing. It was taught in the Old Testament. The Kingdom of God on earth was not new : it was taught in the Old Testament. The " Better Country " was not new, the "Heavenly City," the "New Jerusalem," the "Baptism of the Holy Spirit" were not new. All these were prophetically made known under the Old Testament. For instance, God, through the mouth of the Prophet Joel, promised that in the last days He would " pour out His Spirit upon all flesh " (Joel 2 : 27 ; Acts 2 : 4). But the Body of Christ is called the "Gospel of the Mystery," and Paul calls it "My Gospel." The Church is a distinct organism, a Body, the Body of Christ, consisting of those called out, from among Jews and Gentiles, into that Body. This mystery was in past ages hid in God, but was later revealed to the Apostle Paul, and of it the apostles and prophets are the custodians and exponents.

ENTRANCE INTO THE BODY OF CHRIST
(I Cor. 12 : 13)

The entrance into the Body of Christ is by the Baptism of the Holy Spirit. It is generally believed that everyone who is born again is in the Body of Christ. According to this, the Old Testament saints are in the same category as the New Testament saints. It must be understood that there is a distinct difference between the Old and New Testament

economy, inasmuch as the Holy Spirit had not been poured
out under the old economy, which was the dispensation of
the Father.   Not until Jesus was glorified was the Holy Spirit
thus given.   The Holy Spirit was operative in Old Testament
times, but the purpose was different and His activities were
restricted in certain directions.   During the dispensation of
God the Father, the Holy Spirit pointed to the Coming of
Christ, the Son.   But the Body of Christ is revealed in
the dispensational setting of the Holy Spirit in the New
Testament.   Its formation started at the outpouring of the
Holy Spirit on the Day of Pentecost, whilst believers entered
into the Kingdom under the old economy by the very act
of the New Birth.   And the order has not changed.   We
are born into the Kingdom, and baptized into the Body.
The Apostle states clearly that " we are baptized by one
Spirit into one Body " (I Cor. 12 : 13).   Notwithstanding the
numerous evidences which the Scriptures give of the dis-
tinctiveness of the Baptism of the Spirit, evidences which
only blind people could fail to see, a large section of the
Lord's people still maintain that the New Birth and the
Baptism of the Holy Spirit are one and the same, or that
they are received together.   The Baptism of the Holy Spirit
is only for those who are already born again, bringing with
it an inward consciousness and evidence that Christ has made
His abode in the heart.   It is also the work of the Holy Spirit
to locate every member in the Body of Christ.

MINISTERS OF GOD

What we need today are ministers after God's own heart,
saved and sanctified.   One danger of any movement is to
have ministers who are unsaved, unholy, unsanctified.   We
are not to put our trust in man, but we must put our faith
absolutely in the Lord because man at best may fail.   But

while acknowledging that, it must be remembered that the power of any church in the land has been men devoted, consecrated, sanctified and filled with the fire of God. When ministers and leaders are manufactured in the mould of the world, and pushed into office to lead souls to eternity, when they themselves do not know God, the tragedy is great, and there follows no end to the devastation.

FUTURE CALAMITIES

" And I will show wonders in heaven above and signs
in the earth beneath " (Acts 2 : 19, 20)

Awful calamities in the physical world are predicted by Joel. Many commentators put this down to the breaking up of the fabric of world government, and the overthrow of civil and social powers. This has and will happen without doubt, but more will take place. There are certain portents noted by Josephus in his " History of the Jews " at the great Destruction of Jerusalem in 70 A.D., which had been predicted by our Lord. There were terrible convulsions in the realm of nature, terrific thunderings, lightnings, earthquakes, while a fiery comet was seen hanging over the city for a period of time, and a flaming sword above the doomed city was also seen, and some strange light appeared above the Temple. The streets streamed with human blood, while the burning heaps which followed the incendiarism sent up clouds of smoke which hung over the district. The Holy Temple blazed as a torch, and thousands of men and women were nailed against the walls, a ghastly reminder of the treatment meted out by the inhabitants of Jerusalem in former days to the Just One, Whom they nailed to a tree. This was only the shadow of the coming destruction when Joel's prophecy will be fulfilled to the uttermost. The catastrophes which will mark the end of the Age will take place as described in the Book of Revelation.

- - - - - -

Secondly, we will present outlines of and excerpts from the sermons of Pastor W. J. Williams.

NUMBERS 21

1. Rebelling (v. 5).
2. Confessing (v. 7).
3. Progressing (v. 10).
4. Singing (v. 17).
5. Conquering (v. 24).

_____

MEDITATIONS ON THE LAMB OF GOD

Gen. 22 : 8 ; Exod. 12 : 5 ; I Peter 1 : 19 ; John 1 : 29 ; Rev. 5 : 11, 12.
1. The Lamb provided : ' Foreordained before the foundation of the world.'
2. The Lamb proved : ' The Lamb without spot.'
3. The Lamb preached : ' Behold the Lamb of God.'
4. The Lamb praised : ' Worthy is the Lamb.'

_____

JESUS CHRIST (Rev. 1 : 5-7)

1. Lover of our souls : ' Loved us.'
2. Cleanser of our souls : ' Washed us.'
3. Ennobler of our souls : ' Kings and Priests.'
4. Hero of our souls : ' Unto Him.'
5. Hope of our souls : ' Behold He cometh.'

_____

THE LAMB OF REVELATION

1. The Worth of the Lamb (Rev. 5 : 9).
2. The Wrath of the Lamb (Rev. 6 : 15-17).
3. The Blood of the Lamb (Rev. 7 : 13, 15, 16).
4. The Book of the Lamb (Rev. 13 : 8).
5. The Song of the Lamb (Rev. 15 : 3).
6. The Marriage of the Lamb (Rev. 19 : 9).

7. The Supper of the Lamb (Rev. 19 : 9).
8. The Light of the Lamb (Rev. 21 : 23).
9. The Throne of the Lamb (Rev. 22 : 3, 4, 11).

HE IS RISEN (Acts 1 : 1-11)

1. Proof of the Resurrection (v. 3).
2. Promise—The Resurrected One (v. 4).
3. Person promised (v. 5).
4. Purpose—Witnessing (v. 8).
5. Pathway of Witnessing. Uttermost parts (v. 8).
6. Parting from Jesus (v. 9).
7. Prediction about Christ (v. 11).

RESURRECTION (Acts 1 : 1-11)

1. Eye Proof—Empty Grave (v. 3).
2. Ear Proof—Speaking of the things pertaining to the Kingdom of God (v. 3).
3. Touch Proof (Luke 28 : 39, 40).
4. Ministerial Proof (John 20 : 19, 20, 21).

HANDS OF JESUS

1. Hands of Toil (Matt. 13 : 55).
2. Hands of Bounty (John 6 : 12).
3. Hands of Healing (Matt. 11 : 5).
4. Hands of Help (Matt. 14 : 30, 31).
5. Hands that were pierced (Psalm 22 : 16).

THE VISION OF THE CROSS (Isaiah 53)

1. The Suffering Saviour (1-3).
2. The Sufficient Saviour (4-6).
3. The Submissive Saviour (7-10).
4. The Satisfied Saviour (11-12).

FIRST MIRACLE AFTER PENTECOST (Acts 3 : 1-10)

1. The Partners—Peter and John.
2. The Petitioner—The Beggar.
3. The Power—Of the Apostles.
4. The People—They saw him.

WHAT IS AFTER DEATH ? (Luke 16 : 22-24)

1. There is Existence.
2. There is Sight.
3. There is Torment.
4. There is Prayer.
5. There is Memory.
6. There is a Great Gulf.

THE WALK OF THE BRIDE (Song of Solomon 8 : 5)

1. Place of Walk : Wilderness.
2. Position of Walk : Leaning on her Beloved.
3. Pattern of Walk : Found Him.
4. Power of Walk : Fellowship.

A HELPMEET

"I will make him an helpmeet for him " (Gen. 2 : 18)

1. A Helpmeet in Prayer.
2. A Helpmeet in Praise.
3. A Helpmeet in Practice.

DUTIES AND PRIVILEGES OF WOMEN

1. Woman's relationship to her Home.
2. Wife's relationship to her Husband.
3. Woman's relationship to Social Life.
4. Woman's relationship to the Church.

ESTHER (Esther Chapters 3, 4, 8)

1. The Problems of Opportunities.

2. The Peril of Opportunities.
3. The Privilege of Opportunities.
4. The Productiveness of Opportunities.

WOMAN OF SAMARIA (John 4)

1. Her Character : Sinner.
2. Her Condition : Samaritan.
3. Her Controversy : Found out.
4. Her Conviction : Believed.
5. Her Confession : Preached.
6. Her Conquest : Souls saved.

HOPE OF HIS CALLING

1. Hope of Israel (Gen. 12 : 2).
2. Hope of the Gentiles (Ephs. 3).
3. Hope of the Church (Phil. 3 : 20).

UNITY OF EPHESIANS

1. Plea to keep Unity (Ephs. 4 : 3).
2. Possibility of Unity (Ephs. 4 : 13, 14).
3. Process of Unity (Ephs. 4 : 7-12).
4. Purpose of Unity (Ephs. 2 : 7).

THE WALK OF THE CHRISTIAN

1. Walk Worthy (Ephs. 4 : 1).
2. Walk in Unity (Ephs. 4 : 4-12).
3. Walk not as the Gentiles (Ephs. 4 : 17).
4. Walk in Love (Ephs. 5 : 2).

THE ANOINTED LIFE

1. Love Life (I Cor. 13).
2. Fragrant Life (Psalm 45 : 8).
3. Joyous Life (Phil. 4 : 4).
4. Illuminated Life (I John 2 : 27).

5. Active Life (Acts 1 : 8).
6. Preserved Life (Psalm 23 : 5).

———

BESEECHING

1. Confession (II Cor. 5 : 20).
2. Consecration (Rom. 12 : 1).
3. Continuation (II Cor. 6 : 1).

———

CHRISTIAN PARTAKERS

1. Partakers of Christ's Life (II Peter 1 : 4).
2. Partakers of Christ's Suffering (I Peter 4 : 13).
3. Partakers of Christ's Glory (I Peter 5 : 1).

———

MISSIONARY LIFE

1. Living Adventurously : Heroes of Faith.
2. Living Adaptably : Adapt oneself to surroundings.
3. Life Altruistically : Be devoted to the need of others.

———

WHAT CHURCH TO ATTEND

The question has been asked in our days : " If God gave you light in the Church, why did you not stay in it, and let your light shine among them ?" But what if they do not believe in Baptism in Water and the Baptism of the Holy Spirit ? Surely that congregation, if they did not believe in these ordinances and blessings, would not want us to remain. I remember my father once in a company of people. They were asking this question and one person in the company said : " I believe that everyone should stay in the place where they had the ' light '." My father answered : " If that is logical and right, I should have stayed in bed all my life, because it was there I was saved !"

REPENTANCE

The first message the Apostolic Church should give to the world, is : "Repent, that your sins be blotted out." Repentance means contrition of heart and being sorry for your sins. It also includes confession of sin, not to any mere man, but to God. The only sin that is forgiven is confessed sin. But it goes further than that, it involves conversion and amendment of life, and turning from sin to serve the Living God. We must be careful lest we make the way of salvation too easy for those who listen. Jesus preached repentance, His disciples preached it, and we must preach it. We must not coax people to come to Christ, but show them the grossness and heinousness of sin, and their evil condition because of their sin, but if they will repent and prostrate themselves on their faces in sackcloth and ashes and cry for forgiveness they will be saved.

EXAGGERATION

One outstanding characteristic of a Christian's life must be truthfulness. He must be accurate in his statements from the pulpit or platform, as well as elsewhere. There is a tendency in us by nature to exaggerate concerning results, conversions, healings and baptisms. God's miracles will stand the test of any critic without boasting about them. There is no need to exaggerate in regard to any special miracle that takes place, or in regard to the number of people who are healed. The facts will speak for themselves as they did in New Testament times. Again, if a few are saved some Christians magnify the number, but there is no need, there is great joy in heaven even if one is saved. We are, after all, not following the Lord because of healings and blessings, but because the truth of God has taken hold of our innermost beings.

HUMILITY AND BOLDNESS

The character of John the Baptist was composed of two characteristics at least, humility and boldness. Righteous indignation against sin is not inconsistent with humility. John was very humble, he had no home, and was very poor, but he rebuked Herod the King on his throne. He would not compromise with sin. Yet he was humble. When all Jerusalem came out to the wilderness, the Priests and Levites came to ask : " Who are you, John ?" He might have said, " I am a great preacher, with vast crowds coming to hear me !" But John did not say that. He said : " I am a voice crying in the wilderness, Prepare ye the way of the Lord. The One Who cometh after me is preferred before me, I am unworthy to unloose the latchets of His shoes." That was John's testimony. Do we take that attitude today when God is using us mightily, or do we take the glory to ourselves ?

CHRIST'S INCARNATION
" A Body has Thou prepared Me "

Christ took upon Him a body prepared by God. It could not have been otherwise. He could not serve and accomplish His purpose apart from this prepared body. Only in such a sinless body could be made the great sacrifice for sin. A body coming into existence by the natural processes of generation would be sinful and unholy. His human body came into existence by the creative power of the Holy Spirit. If it had not been a prepared body, it would have been a body of sin, in which the fallen nature of man would have been present. Who can bring a clean thing out of an unclean ? He could not have offered a sinful body by the Eternal Spirit of God. The death of that body would have been like the death of every human body, the result of sin. Sin gives death a claim on our bodies. On a sinless body death can have no claim. Christ, as to His humanity, was absolutely sinless. Upon this point it is of the utmost importance to be very clear and sound, for error as to the Person of Christ is so fundamental that it is sure to invalidate in the end every doctrine of the Gospel.

———

PARTAKERS OF THE DIVINE NATURE

It is most essential for us to understand and realize and believe this truth. Concerning our condition by nature we are dead in trespasses and sin. There is not a spark of Divine life in any of us outside Christ. Not one child of Adam possesses eternal life. All are impure, corrupt, defiled, depraved, debased. The bent of our nature is towards sin. "He that is in the flesh cannot please God." "The carnal mind is at enmity against God." Thus it is absolutely necessary for us to receive new life and to be born again. We are not Christians by our first birth, we are such only by the New Birth. Man only becomes a Christian when he personally approaches the Author and Fountain of life. Christ said : "I am come that ye might have life and have it more abundantly." And this Christian life will reveal a radical revolutionary change in the core and centre of our beings.

———

REVIVAL

We can all talk, criticize, even condemn things in the Church, saying the work is not the same as it used to be. We should remember that there cannot be a revival in the work, or the Church, if the individual is not revived. The work depends upon the spirit of the people. The Revival must be worked in before it can be worked out, worked down before it can be worked up. What can the prayer of revived people accomplish ? The possibilities are limitless and enormous.

WHAT HAPPENS AFTER DEATH ?

Some people may ask : " What does the Apostolic Church believe about the hereafter ? Does it believe in a second chance in the next life ?" We very definitely say No ! The only opportunity that sinners have to be saved is in this life. " Now is the accepted time ; now is the day of salvation." Some state that God is a God of love, and merciful ; and He is, as He has shown on Calvary. But we must remember that God is just and righteous as well, and He must punish sin. I was holding a week's Special Mission in one place, and at the end of one service a man came to me and said : " Mr. Williams, I have come to tell you that God does not love me, and I am going to Hell with no hope. I have not slept for seven nights, and if I do not sleep tonight I must make an end of my life." I answered : " What seems to you hard and unkind is where I see the love of God. You think God is unfeeling and is not allowing you to sleep because you are unsaved. I believe that God loves you so much that He has kept you awake for seven nights that you might realize that you are not saved." " Is there hope for me ?" he asked. " Yes," I replied, " and if you will repent and believe in the Lamb of God, He will save you now." Down on our knees we went, and he was saved, and he went home with his face shining with the glory of God. How glad we are that Jesus saves on this earth, but He never saves in Hell. If you neglect so great a salvation now, how shall you escape the wrath of God ?

READINESS FOR CHRIST'S COMING

We do not know when Christ is coming, it may be tonight, it may be tomorrow, but this we are sure of—He **is** coming

Yet we must be ready for His coming, as Christ is coming
for those who are watching, waiting and looking for Him.
How can we expect to be ready if we have quarelled with
our wife or husband, or if we are not in harmony with our
brother or sister in the Lord.   When He comes, He will take
the pure in heart to Himself, and he that hath this hope in
Him purifieth himself, even as He is pure.   Everyone will not
be in the Bride.   John the Baptist will be present at His
coming, but he will not be in the Bride, for the Scriptures
declare that He is the friend of the Bridegroom.   He will
have many blessings in the future.   Think of the contrast
between his past life and his future life.   He had the wilderness here, but he will have a paradise up yonder.   He ate
locusts here and wild honey was his food, but by-and-by he
will be at the marriage feast.   He had camel's hair for his
dress here, but one day he will be able to say

> With our wedding garments on,
> We shall meet the loved ones gone,
>   At the great Marriage Supper of the Lamb.

But, being the friend of the Bridegroom, He will only be the
' Best Man ' at the marriage.   At the Marriage Supper will
be the Bridegroom, Christ, the Bride, whom many believe to
be the Church, and the guests, John the Baptist, and others
like him.

> Oh !   Can you say you are ready, brother,
>   Ready for the soul's bright home ?

CHAPTER THIRTEEN

PROPHETIC EXPOSITION

A UNIQUE feature in the Apostolic Church Conventions is the prophetical ministry that flows through the Prophets, and the exposition of the prophetic word given to the congregations. Certain excerpts from the prophecies through Pastor W. J. Williams have been inserted in this chapter, and afterwards the corresponding expository observations upon the same passages. Without such expositions given in the Conventions the majority of the congregations listening would have gone away without full enlightenment as to the substance of the word.

Some of our readers will not have had the opportunity of hearing these prophecies and those through other prophets, and the expositions offered by Pastor D. P. Williams, when he was convener of the International Convention at Penygroes. No doubt, therefore, they will appreciate the following prophecies and expositions. Because of limitations of space the abstracts have regrettably had to be somewhat abridged.

THE GREATNESS OF GOD

Prophetical Ministry

" Let every heart be tuned inwardly to the revelation of My will at the commencement of your gathering. What is the revelation at the present moment ? What is the need ? You differ in your need, but before your need can be met you must know that your God is Great. Let this be the supreme theme of your gathering, ' Great is our God, and greatly to be praised.' Do not measure your God by what you have experienced. Do not measure Him by what you have understood of Him. Do not measure your God by that which you have seen, even by that which He has wrought in your midst. You are not great enough to know of My greatness, but give an opportunity for My Spirit to reveal My greatness within your midst.

" I know your disposition and condition, and that you have come into My presence, trying to find a solution to meet the demands of your need, and your life, instead of finding God. He is the answer to the problems of your lives. He is the answer to the situation in whatever condition you are found. The answer is God. The challenge was : ' Whose god is he that can deliver ?' Our God ! Our God ! Our God ! It was not their deliverance that was in sight, there was something involved greater than the deliverance of men from the fire.

" The question that day was playing upon the activities of Jehovah, even in the rejection of that which was commenced since the foundation of the world. There is a movement in the will of Jehovah that must take place down through the centuries. But I would have you to remember this, that something has been commenced before the foundation of the world. You can benefit much in the establishment in that which was commenced since the foundation of the world. There are infallible promises that are working at this present moment even in the heart of the Chosen Nation of the Lord your God. Yet the activities of My Greatness are enough to meet the demands of you individually, and as families. I would have you to remember that these demands have been met through the ages, whether Jew or Gentile in the realm of My will and My care.

" But I am in the midst now, not speaking of an outward Chosen Nation, but speaking in the midst of something that commenced before the foundation of the world. And it is here that the glory of My power and the greatness of My purposes and will are going to be displayed, and in that orb, in that sphere and purpose you have found yourselves at the present time. I would have you to revel in the truth that you are in a higher realm, and it is the greatness of your God that is going to be sufficient to meet the demands in this realm, I am great, and greatly to be praised, Saith the Lord."

Prophetic Exposition

" The keynote of the Convention, as you have heard through the Prophet, is the Greatness of our God. We read in one place in the Book of Acts that ' they spake with tongues, and magnified God.' I was passing near a station the other day, and I looked into a magnifying glass, and I was surprised to see how large I was, with a round face. Well, there is the same in operation on the people that are open to the Holy Spirit to work upon them. They have seen God in His Greatness, and they magnify Him.

" The Lord referred to the great challenge of that Monarch down in Babylon, Nebuchadnezzar, when the three young striplings were bound hand and foot together and thrown into the fiery furnace. He said : ' Who is that god that is able to deliver from My hands ?' But the Lord told us that it was not their deliverance merely that was in view with God. There was something greater than that. Their deliverance was only a token of God's intention to deliver His Own nation out of the furnace of captivity. The bringing out of the three boys was a type of the bringing out of the whole nation together. The three Hebrew lads trusted in that Great God that was able to deliver, and yet they said : ' If He will not deliver us, He will remain just as great in our eyes. He will not be a smaller God even if we burn to ashes ; He will always be Great.' So the challenge of this King to the Greatness of Jehovah concerned His movements ' from the foundation of the world.'

" The Scriptures tell us of movements established from the

foundation of the world, movements which are, of course, earthward, the earthward movements of time.   But there are three things in the Scripture that started, if they ever did start, before the foundation of the world.   Jesus said in John 17 : ' Thou hast loved Me before the foundation of the world.'   When do you think God started to love His Son ? Then the Scriptures tell us that the Lord Jesus Christ was ordained before the foundation of the world to redeem the Church.   Again the Bible says, that we were predestinated before the foundation of the world.   He has a plan from the foundation of the world, in relation to the Jewish nation, which is earthward.   It is a great plan in relation to His chosen nation, and in regards to the Land of Israel.   But He has a tremendously greater plan in relation to His purposes before the foundation of the world in electing us in Jesus Christ.

" There is no commencement of His love towards His Son, and there is no commencement of His love towards His Church in the eternal plan of God.   He has formulated a plan to have a Church, not to be established as an earthly nation from the foundation of the world, but to inherit the Eternal ages with Him in the Heavenly Places.   But there will be a challenge to the Jews and to the Church.   The Jewish nation are on the verge of the last onslaught that will take place from the challenge of the Anti-Christ, the last Monarch.   There is, however, a higher challenge, the Gates of Hell will challenge the Church.   Lucifer and all the infernal hosts are challenging the work designed before the foundation of the world, but they shall never destroy or conquer it, the holy predetermined plan of a glorified Body, of which Christ is the Head."

THE ATTACKS OF SATAN
Prophetical Ministry
" Remember this, the Adversary is present, and has been

from the beginning. He has presented himself in the Feast before Me. He has been the accuser in the unseen silent realms of My presence in your midst. And I would have you to remember that he rebels furiously, and he refuses to acknowledge defeat. He rejects that which I have done in your hearts. Be not surprised at this, for even after being chained for the thousand years, he will not acknowledge even there while chained, for the first thing he will do after he is released, will be to gather again the forces together for a desperate attack to try and defeat the One Who has conquered all. If this be true in the Dispensational sense, when the winding up of the Millennial Age shall take place, be not surprised when you will find him roaring, and twisting in the grass and hissing his poisonous preparations against that which I have inwrought in your hearts, and in the midst of you.

"He will attack the mental realm, the physical and the spiritual realm, and with a definite purpose to destroy that which has been accomplished. He will watch you individually in the hope of being able to conquer and to overcome you. Elijah wanted to die, and in the despondency of his condition, saw defeat, but there is no defeat. If you will believe My word there is no defeat for the individual any more than for the congregation. I am able to protect you, and to give the victory, if you trust in My unfailing promise.

"How can you preserve yourselves ? Be active in praising still, when alone, be active in obeying still, when alone. Let the enthusiasm created by My Spirit in your hearts collectively respond to the claims of Jehovah in your lives when ye are found alone. Allow the Divine principles of the spiritual life to be incarnated in your life. Act them ; let all know that at any cost, whatever the cost may be to you individually, you are going forth in the might of My word, to overcome. Abase yourselves, if needs be, to accomplish the Will of God in the different realms of life. I want you to believe My word. There is no defeat, Saith the Lord."

Prophetic Exposition

" God is great in the lonely life of the individual, where the Devil tries to slay us. In our assembling together, where there is song and prayer and ministry, Satan fails to accomplish his purpose in slaying us, but he has one purpose, that what God has said in the Church shall not be fulfilled. The individual plays a part with the collective whole in gaining victory in God's will throughout the year. With all kinds of insinuations and suggestions, Satan tries to cause the individual to lose God, and thus manages to overcome the collective whole.

" There are battles in the home life, the assembly life, the district life, the national life. There are certain evil angelic hosts and princes fighting against certain nations, not the same against Wales as against Scotland or Nigeria. Satan has arranged his kingdom in such a way as to fight the children of God in these nations. He attacks first the individual, and if you conquer as an individual in your ' alone ' battle, he tries in the assemblies to kill the weak ones. He attacks the flesh and causes members of the Church to be disappointed, or to be insulted, or offended, or causes them to grumble and find fault with others in order to kill their faith.

" Do you know that there have been demons here from all parts of the world fighting in this Convention ? There is a perfect strategy in the Infernal Kingdom against the reigning life in the saints. Satan knows that we are saved. He is not fighting me as far as salvation is concerned. But if he can he would have you and me as tools in his hands to frustrate the reigning power of Christ in your life. The Lord said that after the prophets of Baal were slaughtered on

Mount Carmel, Elijah went under a juniper tree, and later into the cave. One of the angels of glory came with a loaf of cake ready-made from Heaven's bakehouse for him. A similar battle came to my experience last year, when Pastor Brownlie came to my assistance, while I was groaning and weeping, and the pressure of the Devil, and the weight of the infernal battle was crushing me.

" We cannot effectively combat this great power that is against us, but as we yield ourselves to the victory of the Cross, count by faith always that Satan is a conquered foe. The government of Hell is against the government of the Church, but let us war a good warfare, and we shall be victorious. Yet Satan will not acknowledge our victory. After a thousand years spent in chains in the bottomless pit, the first thing he will do will be to come out of the abyss and strike against the City of the Most High, and he will try to slaughter even the saints of the New Jerusalem in great fury, in order to have his kingdom again. But at that moment the Fire will come down and it is the Fire that comes down that creates victory all the time."

HEALTHY CHRISTIANS
Prophetical Ministry

" Remember the foundation of the Feast, the Three-in-One, the One-in-Three. If you have guarded perfectly your faith, in this respect your safety hath been sealed by Me. It is not necessary to give your ears to the warnings of men, nor to the warnings of spirits. What I desire is that ye believe in My will and My plan on your behalf, that operates to bring you wholly into connection with Myself.

" Great is your cry to obtain bodily blessings. I desire you to be separated from all that look unto Me merely for a natural blessing. I hear the cry of humanity enquiring what they shall drink, and what they shall eat, and wherewithal they shall clothe themselves. I have given a reply plainly in My word, that I am able to clothe, to sustain the lily that perisheth. My word explains this to you.

" A healthy body—this blessing has been assured unto you. But hearken, ten were cleansed, but only one remained steadfast. And ye will be unable to remain steadfast, in the power of natural blessing, in the midst of the crushing might of the predestined moments, when the demands of the throne of the Lord God call upon you to remain faithful unto Him. The demands of the world, and its needs, eat up your natural blessings, your time, and your all, stealing your affections from the Lord your God. Consequently I touch you, and give you that blessing of bodily health ; yet I say unto you, ye will not have a multitude to follow Me according to the mystery of the preordained plan, in virtue of a physical health blessing. There are still nine living unto themselves, using up selfishly the strength imparted to them. It is only one stranger that hath remained faithful. The stranger (Luke 17 : 17, 18) it is whom I use according to the mystery of the preordained Covenant of Peace.

"Others have received a soul blessing. A vision, a revelation, a blessing has been received by the soul of some. But this is what the soulish blessing does to the multitude today. When someone whom I am using is encountered, those that exist upon the soulish realm would restrain those whom I use elsewhere, because they don't belong to you. Schismatic divisions are brought into being as a result of living upon soulish blessings, and soul truths. I continue to ask : ' Who is Paul, and who is Apollos ?' Therefore, if what you have received is a blessing appealing to the human affections, a soulish revelation, you will only be a means to thwart and run counter to the intentions of the predestinated mystery, for ye will cause divisions to arise in your midst, you will draw disciples after you. But such people will never do any harm to the predestined plan of the Lord God, for the lovers sought by all who are soulishly affectioned will die, but He Who is loved by the spirit hath already died, and behold He is alive for evermore.

" I desire to come into the innermost sanctuary of your beings in order to deal with your spirits. Before ye are able to grip the preordained revelation in the realm of the spirit, the soulish must be controlled by the spiritual and the body be subjugated to the perfections of the Infinite God, and you become submissive to Me in your spirit. When you are possessed in the realm of the spirit, according to My word, you shall then choose the doing of My will in perfectness, Saith the Lord."

Prophetic Exposition

" From the commencement of the Convention the Lord has been speaking strongly on the need of holiness and sanctification. He wants to cleanse the environment of your soul. He wants to impart into every heart the principles of truth and righteousness. That is the only way to healthy homes. We can be very robust in body, in a grand physical condition, with good sinews and arteries, but our hearts foul and corrupt, the environment of our conversation, and our language, our opinions, and our desires, and inclinations unhealthy. But He has come to make us a healthy people, with healthy minds.

" Some diseases are contagious. You keep away from a consumptive person ; you are afraid of the germs. There are consumptive souls, full of germs of evil thoughts and malice and hatred and backbiting, and when you converse with them they impart and imbue evil germs into your mind and thoughts, and you become polluted. But Christ is the environment of your souls, and He keeps us healthy as we commune and live with Him. As He is able to do that with

the individual, so also with an assembly, that the assembly
may be full of health. A holy stream will then go out from
the Church of God, as an environment to the world outside,
full of sweetness and radiancy.

" Dealing with the healing of the body, after referring to
the ten lepers who were healed, and the one who remained,
the Divine thought given us was, that you can never have a
congregation of people to follow and go through with the
Lord and to carry out His eternal predestinations because
of an outward miraculous demonstration of the healing of
their bodies. It is only a divine revelation to the spirit, and
a personal knowledge of God that will do it. They that move
on a material, physical or psychical plane of truth will fail ;
they will not return to the Lord with thanksgiving, but they
that have the spiritual conception will do the will of God.

" The elements that are in the nature and life of those that
have only a soulish revelation always forbid others to do
great things for God. ' We saw someone casting out demons,'
they told the Lord of old, and ' we told him not to do so,
because he was not one of our company.' That was a sign,
the Lord said, that their revelation was soulish. There was
selfishness beneath it. It was a creed that wanted to keep
the Christ within their little borders, but Christ is universal,
and He touches the universe. It is a sin when you forbid
others to do great things in His Name. The point to me is :
Am I with Him ? Does He use me ? If I am doing His
will, He will look after everybody else.

" Again, if your revelation is spiritual, you will not count
your life dear to you, and you will not be disobedient to the
heavenly vision. Paul had a personal revelation from the
third heaven, Paradise. He said : ' I did not receive it from
man, I received it from God.' In one place he goes so far
as to call the revelation ' My Gospel.' It was so personal
God gave it to him. He claimed it as his, and the respon-

sibility rested upon him to remain faithful unto God. He counted not his own life dear unto him. Involved in that revelation to Paul's spirit, and embodied in the Divine Commission to every Christian is the principle of self-denial and self-surrender to the will of God. Consequently there is a participation in the sufferings of Christ."

JESUS CHRIST IS LORD AND SUPPLIES OUR NEED

Prophetical Ministry

" Before the end of the Convention many will feel : ' I am so small ; no one sees me ; no one knows that I am here.' But I have seen everyone, and I want everyone to be encouraged by the fact that he is under My supervision. Let there be no disappointment in that respect because I give a portion to all while they are in My presence. Of old they went a day's journey without noticing that He was not among them. At that time He was among the ' unnoticeable.' He was only a child, they never thought there was anything important about Him. I have come to this Convention to meet the ' unnoticeable,' and they that are noticeable, the poor and the rich, the unwise and the wise.

" I say unto you that there is a larger congregation pressing upon Me at this hour than there are present here. Even the nations of the world are pressing upon Me at this time. Why ? Because there is no other Person but Myself that has been ordained to meet the demands of the nations. The streaming virtue will flow out of My Person to heal all who will touch Me, for no one has pressed towards Me without receiving that healing virtue. The completeness of the Trinity in the Godhead has today a life-giving, virtuous, Divine, self-existent stream which is well able to supply the need of all. There is a great multitude at this time pressing on Me to try to crush Me out of existence, Saith the Lord."

Prophetic Exposition

" I will try to be brief while explaining what God the Holy Spirit has been telling us. The Lord desires to give us all assurance that not one has come to the Convention without being under His notice. His foster-father, Joseph, and His mother, Mary, went a day's journey thinking that He was among the crowd. Although ' unnoticeable,' He was at that very moment with the ' noticeable.' He was with the doctors. This word is to encourage the ' unnoticeable,' or any who may feel thus in the Convention. We are to remember that God is the Governor of the Feast and will supply the needs of all.

" The prophecy then went on to speak of the woman who pressed through the crowd and touched the hem of Christ's garment, and was healed. Her need was met and so can ours be. But notice the pregnant phrase : ' There is also a great multitude at this time pressing on Me to try and crush Me out of existence.' Listen ! Apostolic brethren and all other brethren in the Lord, we have arrived at a crisis in the history of theology, or in the history of the opinions of people with regard to the Person of our Lord Jesus Christ. If we have only come to this Convention to declare to everyone present that Jesus Christ is God, let all know that we believe that Christ Jesus the Lord, the King of Glory, is God eternal.

" One of the greatest theologians of Wales (he is a creator of ministers), at his University is passing ministers out through a materialistic machine. He said the other day that he did not know where to place the Second Person in the Trinity. He could not find a place for Him among humanity, He was so unique above all human beings. But, on the other hand, he could not find a place for Him in the Godhead. But we as Apostolic saints have come here to declare that we have found a place for Him in the Godhead, Christ is God, the Second Person in the Trinity." (The congregation voiced their approval of the President's assertion by a loud and continuous shout of assent). " Now I venture to say that that shout is not superficial. There is something in that voice that shatters Hell, because the great strategy of the infernal hosts is to crush Jesus Christ, the Son of God, out of existence, but He liveth for ever." (Exultant applause from all the saints).

THE GREAT PHYSICIAN

Prophetical Ministry

" I am jealous. If you declare, My people, that you desire to hear My voice, I will respond ; but I am jealous. Let My voice in response to your prayer touch you. Welcome into My presence, for I am the friend of sinners, not because of sin, but because I can help you not to sin, because I am desirous of delivering you from sin, and that you may have fellowship with Me at all times. Welcome to My presence, even as you are, for there is not one that can claim worthiness to come to My presence, but all are welcome, because I am here to meet your expectations.

" If you are blind, I am come to give you sight. Be not too occupied with the natural, with the physical, when you hear the word invitation and welcome, but understand the divine principle and the desires of My heart for one and all to see as I see. I am desirous to give you spiritual sight so that you may see as I see. Then what a transformation. It is because you are blind that oft-times you are causing Me trouble. When I am speaking, coming in tenderness and compassion, telling you that I do love you, and desirous of having you for Myself. When I am revealing the mystery of the programme of the future unto you, and when the purposes of the future are unveiled, oft-times ye do say : ' I cannot see,' but I am come to give sight to the blind. I declare that I would be more glorified during this holy convocation to know that every one of you see as I see, even more than to be able to see in the natural sense.

" Some are lame, as well, but I am come to make the lame leap, and to walk according to My will. Think not of lameness in the natural, in the physical realm. Many of you have been lame spiritually, and you know it. But I have given you a welcome to My presence, not because you are lame, but because I am able to make you leap with joy.

" Some of you are sick at heart. This sickness is incurable as far as the human possibilities are concerned. But be not over-anxious, and troubled. Though I am here to meet the demands of the physical realm, I am definitely giving you a welcome, so that I may give you sight, so that I may heal your lameness, and touch your disease, that you may be whole spiritually.

" I definitely again say, that there is no worthiness in you to be found to claim liberty of entrance into My presence, but you are welcome as you are, and I will heal. What is the reason that I am anxious to heal you ? The reason is that I want you for Myself. The groanings are heard definitely these days, but I am going to answer the groanings that cannot be uttered in the New Creation in the three aspects. But I am touching the discords of humanity. Yet humanity cannot hold back ; it is My Spirit that holdeth back. There is no hope for the strength of the human to counteract the power of the Infernal. But I am holding back for your sake, Saith the Lord."

Prophetic Exposition

" In II Cor. 3 : 14, we read : ' But their minds were

blinded.' The Lord had been speaking about blindness. Paul deals in this chapter with the blindness that has fallen upon Israel. The message the Lord gave to us was that He had to open our eyes. He strongly emphasised first of all that He was jealous. Think of the yearning of the husband, disappointed with his wife. She had brought about a ruined home, such a disaster to peace, and pleasantness and love when the husband and wife have broken their vows and have grieved one another. Think of the wrench of their love, the husband bleeding because his wife has been trampled under foot by other men. How many times do we read in the Word of God that God is grieved with the harlotry of Israel ? I wonder whether there is a child of God who at some time entered into an oath, tearfully and sincerely with God, and who has by this time drifted away from Him ? Your heart has become cold, you have been carried away by the spirit of the Age. God says that He is jealous. He wants to have you back to Himself completely, so that the world and the Devil will not have an inch of your life any longer. He says : ' I am jealous to have you all to Myself.'

" He welcomes us to His presence, so that we may see the programme of the future. God only knows that programme. If Europe would know her future tonight, beforehand, she would be wailing in dust and ashes. But she is blind to the future. But the Holy Spirit is with us, the word of ministry is with us, and we can see the future, and we have come to see clearer and farther than ever before. Let us ask Him again to bathe our eyes, the eyes of our inner man, with love. Shall we ask Him quietly : ' Bathe me, Lord. Bathe my eyes that I may see. Let the solution be applied to my vision, that I may see clearer than ever.'

" He hears our groaning, for there is a fear in the heart of man, because the power and strength of man is not enough to hold back the spirit of the Infernal hosts. The League of Nations and the Councils of Peace, politically, industrially and commercially, world-wide, since the days of the Great War (1914-1918), have been at it trying to put up a wall against Hell. The leaders, the workers, and the governments of the world feel the force of Devilry, which is threatening the life of the nations of the world. Yet we have groaned. God says it is only His Spirit that can be a wall to hold Satan back. Thank God for a wall for a little time, to preserve us from the onslaughts of Hell, in order that the Holy Spirit may carry out the Divine purposes and the Eternal predestinations of God, in gathering His saints together. And when the wall is taken away, we shall be taken away, and then Hell will sweep the earth. ' No, No,' the Lord said, ' humanity has no hope of counteracting the infernal powers. It is My Spirit that holds them back.'

" Then again He repeated the word that we should pray that our eyes may be opened to reality in order to see God, what He is doing, and what is going on in the world, in order that we may be protected. The Spirit of God can operate in power on our physical frame, but He wants to go further than the outward and the external, to permeate deep into our being, to reach us more completely than ever, to the fulfilment of God's purposes among us. Shall we ask Him, whatever the cost : ' Bathe me ; open my eyes ; heal my lameness, and do a work in me that will remain in my soul for eternity "?

THE FUNCTION OF APOSTLESHIP
Prophetical Ministry

" When He ascended, not only did He set at liberty, not only did He destroy the works of the Enemy but ' He led captivity captive,' and He triumphantly conquered all. There is no need henceforth to fear any power. His place is eternally secured, and your redemption in its fulness can be realized according to the operating power of My presence in your midst.

"There are gifts given for the Dispensational need, and for that which is revealed. And the first one given is the apostleship. I want to emphasize this truth, not man given, but apostleship in virtue of the triumphant victory secured, and assured. Also I want you to know that the purpose of that gift of apostleship is to reveal the character of the Omnipotent One, and of the Omniscient One. The attributes of your Jehovah are assailed on every hand ; but I have given a function, so that the Divine may be in operation in the days of the assailing process.

"My wisdom in every realm is assailed. Follow the trend of the Age, and realize and know the downward tendencies that are acting in the human realm, and the assailing of My wisdom. It is only as you will allow the force of My presence in the midst of My Body to reveal and to make manifest, and to confirm Mine eternal wisdom that it will be possible to stem the tide of iniquity.

"My Goodness is assailed. What is your conception of My Goodness ? Are you able to say : ' Yes, God is good ' ? My Goodness is assailed on every hand, but I have gathered you so that you may be able with assurance to declare that not only is My Wisdom unfailing, but that My Goodness is everlasting, and My Mercy is immeasurable. Rejoice, declare with gladness, with no uncertain sound : ' His mercy endureth for ever.' Given is the apostleship to make known the character of the Holy One in your midst. If the apostleship is sent, do not focus your attention on the human activities and conception of that function, but rather let your faith be possessed with the Divine truth—sent."

Prophetic Exposition

" I will comment again on the word given, to remind us

of what God said. After Christ arose, He ascended, and He took a large company with Him, leading captivity captive. He took some of us with Him, in the Divine programme, but we were not very long up there. He drove us back again into captivity, to be His bondslaves forever. He gave gifts unto men, the gifts of the Ascended Lord, and sent them back in the power of divine election. He sent His Gifts from the Throne to prepare this elective Body to go again to the Throne, where He is.

" Notice the first gift, ' He gave some apostles.' And we are to look beyond the human and see the apostleship ? We know one another so well, don't we ? Him and His foster-father they knew—' Is not this the carpenter's Son ?' They only saw the human ancestry. A root out of a dry ground ! There was no comeliness about Him. They did not see God, infinite in glory, incarnate among them. And as He was incarnate then, He is incarnate now in His Body, the Church, in us the carpenters of the Age, even as in the Third Person of the Trinity, the Holy Spirit of God.

" The purpose of the gift of apostleship is to reveal the character of Christ. The Holy Spirit is sent down from heaven, embodied in gifts in divine election to express the character of the Risen Lord in His Kingship, in His Priesthood, and in His Prophethood. The Holy Spirit is here manifesting His character in wisdom. That is one of His attributes. We are living in days when human wisdom is at its zenith. There never was a day in the history of the human race when human wisdom attained so high a place as now in every sphere in the history of humanity. Yet human wisdom, whether in the political, industrial, philosophical, or any other realm in human society has brought only chaos and confusion. Why ? Because the mark of Calvary is not there. They tell us that they are going in for war, and at other times they tell us they are going in for peace. That is human wisdom. We are not going in for peace. We have got it. The League of Nations will not give us peace, although the delegates to it are humanly, undoubtedly, doing their best. But why do they not come to Calvary ? There is only one avenue and way of peace— reconciliation through the Cross of Jesus Christ.

" Then the message of His goodness is assailed. Thank God, for the goodness of God. How unthankful, unkind and unresponsive is humanity to the goodness of God. But His goodness endureth forever. Then the mercy of God. That is another attribute for the apostleship to reveal. Oh, friends, these are cruel days ! The philosophy of the day is this— they will not have the religion of Calvary because it is the religion of slaughter. They are so refined ; they will not have it. And at the same time they can arrange to put the world in a state of carnage, but the Blood has been shed on Calvary. The apostleship in the Body of Christ is to express mercy in the way of Calvary."

FUTURE EVENTS

Prophetical Ministry

" I have not cast away My people. I have two families, but I would have you to understand that I am great enough to hold both in their realms. They are united to the objects of the purposes which I have for them. The one family is like the sands of the sea in number. Though the flowing tide of the sea has hidden them, they will yet come to sight, for the mysterious power of My Own purposes is keeping the entirety of the purposes of My heart together. Consequently, I am working in the sands. The uprising of the billows of the Gentile nations is taking different directions, and its upheaval is antagonistic to Me. But the beautiful band of the Covenant and My promise is like a girdle around this family, for they are My elect. And they will come to sight again out the depths, as of old I brought them out, through the Red Sea, for the ocean waves of every sea must give way before the power of the Covenant of the Lord God.

" I have the stars of Heaven also in My reckoning, but the Great Whale in the sea is coming to sight, seeking to cast them down with his tail. But I have kept and sustained you. Therefore, magnify My Name, knowing that neither My power nor My wealth is less, and they will never be exhausted. I have raised you from the dunghills, from the dust, and from the pits. But I do not raise any from the Pit of Hell. There is no place there to hide, for there hell has no roof. The Rainbow of the Covenant will never be seen above that pit.

" I would have you to know that He that raised you is able to preserve you. It matters not whether ye are with the few or with the many, ye can rejoice in the inward consciousness that I am keeping you. Who but Myself is able to keep you in the firmamental space where I have placed you ? I call you by your names. Awake and open your eyes to a full realization that I have visited you, and that I remain with you. Consequently, it matters not who is against you, Saith the Lord."

Prophetic Exposition

" The word through the prophetical channel is far reaching, demanding that we judge it in the light of the written word and dwell upon it for our edification. The first declaration was that the Lord has not cast away His people, a reference to Israel (Rom. 11 : 1) ; and that He has two families that He cares for, the family of the sand, and the family of the stars, the earthly and the heavenly (Gen. 15 : 5, 22 : 17). He has placed both in their own calling according to the eternal purposes that He has predestinated for them.　Although His people are as the sands of the sea, buried in the deep, covered by the great currents and floods of the sea of humanity and out of sight, nevertheless they will come to sight.

" Israel, by another analogy, has been buried in the grave of the nations, but there is a restoration going on.　It is taking place already (Ezek. 37 : 12-14).　The mysterious power of divine election towards Israel holds them as a nation together for God's future purpose.　He declares that He still works in the sand.　It is known to you the great upheaval of the nations has been likened to a stormy sea, with its roaring tumult and boisterous waves, and the upheaval will continue until it will spue the disobedient Jonah (Israel) out.

" It is evident, by the signs of the times, that the hand of God is in the deep, and however fiercely it will roar in its fury against God, the girdle of His covenant and promise will keep the Elect Nation together.　They will come to sight from the deep even as of old they came through the Red Sea (Ps. 106 : 9 ; Ezek. 14 : 21).　The waves of every sea must give way to the power of Jehovah's covenant.　God told Abraham to look up to the heavens to view the stars, and told him that his seed would be as numberless as they are, the heavenly family.　But let us watch the tail of the sea-monster, it will endeavour to wipe out of the sky some of the stars.

" We are exhorted to give praise to God and to magnify the Name of the Lord, because we have been raised up from the dunghills, and from the dust, and from the pits (I Sam. 2 : 8).　Mark here the emphatic Word of the Holy Spirit : ' I will raise no one from the Pit.'　This is the final doom of the impenitent.　But God is gracious, and will deliver us from going down into the Pit (Job 33 : 24).　There is no refuge in the Pit, and Hell is naked before Him, and destruction hath no covering (Job 26 : 6).　There will never appear any Bow in the firmament of eternity to promise their deliverance. The inhabitants of the Pit will be grovelling in Eternal Darkness. But we are exhorted to rejoice because of our deliverance, and because He is able to keep us as His elect as stars in His firmament. The constellation of the Redeemed will shine for ever.

" Let us turn to the Word to see what it says concerning the restoration of all things. I fail to see in the Bible that the wicked lost will be restored. Neither is there anything concerning the salvation of the Devil and the fallen angels. Let me touch on some verses dealing with the case. Acts 3 : 19 : ' Whom the heavens must receive until the times of the restitution of all things, which God hath spoken through the mouths of His Holy Prophets, since the world began.' This verse from the sermon of Peter is primarily spoken to the Jews. The prophets of old were used to predict future events, concerning the restoration of Israel and the Palestinian Covenant, the Covenant with David and the Kingdom rule. Therefore in Acts 3 : 19, the word ' restitution ' alludes to the Jews, and their restitution at the return of the Lord, whom they crucified and slew.

" In Colossians 1 : 20 and Ephes. 1 : 10 there is no mention of Hell, or of things under the earth. Divine inspiration has carefully stated ' whether they be things in earth or things in heaven.' The sin of the denizens of the underworld has not been atoned for. The blood was not shed for them. In the future the wicked dead shall appear at the Great White Throne, and because their names are not in the Lamb's Book of Life, they shall be cast into the Lake of Fire. In the meantime we must preach salvation as now is the accepted time and now is the day of salvation."

PART VII

ROLL-CALL

CHAPTER FOURTEEN
CLOSING SCENES

WHILE he was Pastor of the Apostolic Church at Edgware, Middlesex, the strain of the ministry of the years began to tell on Pastor W. Jones Williams. His heart was seriously affected and he was admitted to hospital. The end came even sooner than expected. He passed into the nearer presence of Christ on April 15, 1945, aged 53.

Mrs. John Evans, his daughter, has recorded this recollection of the sad occasion : " When I was called to London to see my father in hospital, he said to me what he had told me before, ' Like a ship in an ocean storm, thus is my little life.' When she assured him he would soon be out of hospital, he replied : ' The Lord gave me a hymn when I came in here, 'There is a land of pure delight where saints immortal reign'.' He repeated the hymn right through, adding that he realized the Lord had given him the hymn to prepare him for his Home-call. He asked that the hymn be sung at his funeral.

" Always he kept his watch under his pillow. He never needed an alarm clock, being able to rise at any hour that happened to be necessary. One day, when the nurse was changing the bed, his watch fell to the floor. The nurse said that she was very sorry. ' It's all right, nurse,' he replied. It was taken for repair, and when told it would take a week before it was ready, the Pastor said : ' I shall be in the Big Watch by then, where there will be no need for a watch or time. There everybody will be praising the Lamb for ever '."

After his death the doctors stated that it was the vast amount of work he had undertaken which had caused him to die at that early age. Pastor W. H. Lewis said at the funeral service : " Pastor W. J. Williams did much sacrificial service. He died a martyr for the Word of God. When he finally went to the doctors they all told him : ' You have killed yourself ; you have driven yourself to death.' Some people live to be ninety years of age, but Pastor Williams, dying at fifty-three has lived far longer than many who have lived to the age of ninety, because of the flame and burning passion in his soul."

By his death the Apostolic Church sustained a grievous loss, but his spirit, influence and ministry live on. His lips are silent, but the words that they uttered from the living God will ever be cherished by those who heard them.

At the funeral which took place at the Apostolic Temple, Penygroes, and was presided over by the Acting President, Pastor H. Dawson, then of Glasgow, a last tribute was paid to Pastor Williams's memory on April 20, 1945. A congregation of over one thousand people filled the building. Others who officiated were Pastor T. V. Lewis, and Pastor W. M. Humphrey, General Secretary of the Church at that time. Pastor W. J. Williams had expressed the desire that Jesus would be exalted at his funeral and that there should be nothing mournful.

There were many expressions of appreciation of the services which the servant of God had rendered to the cause worldwide, and very moving were the tributes paid to his memory. Pastor Dawson first spoke with affectionate regard of the deceased minister and expressed sympathy to the mourners. The following Pastors also contributed : Pastors W. M. Humphreys, H. Cousen, D. T. Rennie, J. O. Jones, C. C. Ireson, W. H. Lewis, J. D. Eynon and T. N. Turnbull.

A poem which appears on the last page of the book by

Pastor Williams, " A Good Minister of Jesus Christ," was read by Pastor Dawson at the funeral service. It describes Pastor Williams himself.

> Servant of Christ, stand fast amid the scorn,
>   Of men who little know or love thy Lord,
> Turn not aside from toil, cease not to warn,
>   Comfort and teach. Trust Him for thy reward.
> A few more moments' suffering, and then
> Cometh sweet rest from all thy heart's deep pain.

At the funeral ministers were present from various denominations. They, too, paid tribute to his memory. The Rev. L. B. James said : " When I visited our departed brother in London, little did I think at that time that I would be present at his funeral so soon. I thank God for calling our brother into the ministry. If he died in London, he will never die in Penygroes, as witness this assembly, and the representatives from the various parts of the country here today."

At the end of the service Pastor John Lindsay closed the proceedings with prayer. The body of Pastor W. J. Williams was afterwards interred beside that of his first wife, in the Apostolic Temple Cemetery, Penygroes. A memorial service was held on Sunday, April 22, at which Pastor T. V. Lewis preached from the text : " He was a burning and shining light." Pastor H. Dawson also spoke words of help, comfort and inspiration from the Word of God.

Pastor Williams was survived by his widow, his daughter Mair (Mrs. John Evans), and his son Mark.

Many telegrams of sympathy were received by the bereaved. One from Australia referred to the sense of shock with which the news of the Pastor's death had been received on the other side of the world. Here are its contents : " It is with the deepest regret that this Executive has received the news per the General Secretary of the Home-call of Pastor W. J.

Williams in a London hospital on April 15, 1945. We were greatly shocked by the news, which came so unexpectedly. As he was one of the founders of the Apostolic Church in Great Britain, we had come to look upon him as a principal pillar of the work. Our association with him as a fellow-worker and servant of God has been very closely bound up with the progress of the Church world-wide, as well as that of personal friendship and fellowship. The results of his faith and labours for the Apostolic Vision cannot be fully estimated, and we esteem it a great privilege to have been co-workers with him in the spreading of the Vision, which he with others sought to propagate. Our deepest sympathy and condolence go out to his wife and family in their bereavement, and in a particular and special sense to his brother, Pastor D. P. Williams, President of the Apostolic Church, who we know will feel the loss in a double sense : first of all, his loss of a very dear brother, and secondly his loss of one who has been with him through all his struggles as Founder of the Church, and who has been the mouthpiece of the Lord for His servant. As an Executive, representing this far-flung Commonwealth of Australia, we feel that we can raise no better memorial to the memory of a great man of God, than to stand firm for the Apostolic Vision and to continue to expand the vision that he so valiantly battled for through the hard years of its inception. Our ardent wish is to be rejoined with him, around the throne above, without shame, sorrow, or loss to ourselves, and the vision he loved so well."

In 1947 Pastor D. P. Williams passed away to be with His Lord. In 1945 he and his wife had gone to Canada. These were the years of World War II, when all the shipping was under restrictive control, and it was difficult to book a sailing. Pastor and Mrs. Williams had not sailed many days when alarm bells rang, and they heard the sound of repeated depth charges, which proved that danger was uncomfortably near.

This went on from midnight until the early hours of the morning, when they were told that an enemy U-Boat had been sunk. After that they had a smooth passage until they docked at Halifax on April 18, 1945.

They arrived in Montreal at 11 o'clock the next night, where, despite the lateness of the hour, quite a number of the members of the Church were there to greet them. As they sat down to supper, they asked the Canadian Pastors present if they had received any news of Pastor W. J. Williams, as he was very ill when they left him. Pastor B. J. Noot looked across the table at Pastor B. G. Evans, and said : "George, will you please tell the Pastor?" "Well, Uncle Dan," he said, " Jones has gone home." There was a hush, and a dead silence, and Pastor and Mrs. Williams left the supper untouched, and went to their bedroom. The shock was too much for tears, and that night sleep vanished.

However, early next morning in prayer, the Pastor and his wife fully surrendered all to the Lord in the realization that "the secret things belong to the Lord our God, but the things that are revealed belong to us." The tears flowed, but the bereaved couple were refreshed in God's presence. It was not long after this that Pastor D. P. Williams was himself taken ill, and so seriously that his wife almost gave up hope of his recovery. For seven weeks they were in the " Valley of Achor," but came at last through the " Door of Hope."

From Montreal they travelled to Toronto, where they were warmly received. After a fortnight's rest, they attended the Sunday morning service. The Pastor felt that if he could only sit among the Lord's people he would be strengthened. But it seemed he might faint at any moment. Before the Breaking of Bread, he was moved to give a short testimony and to thank the members of the Church for their prayers. As he did so, the power of God fell on him, making him whole. From that moment he poured himself out in ministry and service in Canada and America.

What a great experience it was for them as, husband and wife, they travelled together many thousands of miles, for they had been so much apart during their married life because of the Pastor's being so often away on Church work. As they went from one assembly to another, their hearts were often encouraged with the results that they saw, for the members of the Church were responsive to the altar call for consecration, while many came out for salvation.

They had been in Canada eleven months when they learnt that their daughter Mair had become gravely ill with tuberculosis, just at a time when she had everything ready to come and join them in Canada. She was in a sanatorium near Birmingham and the doctors gave little hope of her recovery. Naturally speaking, how easy it would have been for them to have returned home, but they realized that they had been sent of God, and they both sought and waited patiently for the Lord's mind to be revealed.

A few days later, learning that their daughter was much better, they left for America. They were in Baltimore, Maryland, when they received a cable asking them to return as Mair was dangerously ill. They still delayed, awaiting the instructions of the Lord. Then, one Saturday morning, they had word from another daughter, pleading with them to return, as Mair was sinking fast.

After a time of waiting on the Lord, they went to the house of Pastor G. B. Evans, where Pastor J. D. Eynon was staying. There Pastor D. P. Williams fell prostrate, pouring out his heart to the Lord, asking Him to reveal His will. Prophetical ministry came through Pastor Eynon as follows : " I have seen desires in you to abide in this land, but I have ordained that your bones shall rest in the soil of your birthplace, and that the end of your responsibility should be where you commenced. My word unto you is that you let no man take your crown, but rather let the falling of your dust into the native soil be in faith, loyalty, and fidelity unto the Cause. I desire you to say amongst the ones you have laboured with : ' I have kept the faith.' Follow close to My Word. I will not say whether your days are few or many."

A strong appeal was made on compassionate grounds, for an early sailing, which was granted. Within two weeks, they sailed on the " Bayans " from Montreal. The Pastor was taken ill on the boat, and it seemed his end was near ; but his wife, remembering the prophetical ministry, knew he was not to die at sea, and they landed in Liverpool in early November, 1946. They arrived at Gorslas, Penygroes, to find Mair sitting up in bed, weeping with joy. Mr. (later Pastor) and Mrs. Dicks, son-in-law and daughter of Pastor and Mrs. D. P. Williams, now felt that they could relax, for the responsibility would no longer be theirs, although they still played a great part, along with others of the family, who, at no little sacrifice to themselves, shouldered the burden with Mrs. D. P. Williams. The Lord graciously spared Mair, allowing her parents to nurse her for three months.

After a few weeks' ministering in various places in Wales, the Pastor was taken ill and confined to bed. While in Canada the previous year, a doctor had warned him that there was a large hole in one lung, and that if the Pastor caught pneumonia again, the end would not be far away. Nevertheless, obedient as ever to the ministry arrangements, he ministered in certain assemblies with great benefit to the Church members. They were delighted to hear his ministry again, and they were deepened in spiritual life and doctrine.

With two members of the household sick, Mrs. Williams had a heavy burden to bear, but others gave her help in her ministry. Often times it was difficult to know which needed the more attention, since both were ill. Yet many happy hours they spent together before each sick person became too ill and weak for enjoyment. They had much in common, especially in composing poetry, and they did this together as long as they were able.

When Mair was almost passing away, she called out : " Dada, Dada, goodbye ! I am going soon." He answered faintly : " Goodbye, my child." He longed to embrace her, and one night the Lord gave him a vision of her in a glorious state, and two angels coming to fetch her. One had a book under his arm, bearing the word "Beautiful." Another night, he had a vision of two angels coming to fetch him. He saw that one carried a book on which was written the word " Love." He also learnt in a vision that he was not to be buried in his own family grave, but in a place that God would show him. He then sent a message to the Temple elders of the Penygroes Church indicating that he would like to see them. Arriving at the house, they were shown into the Pastor's bedroom, where he gave each of them a parting message. He then asked permission of the elders to be buried in the centre of the plot on the right side of the path leading to the Temple right wing. They promised to grant it, and this was later fulfilled.

He expressed a desire to see all the children and his wife. He gave all the children many words of counsel and wisdom, and a parting word to each one, and then wished them all goodbye. To his dear wife he said : " God be with you ; underneath are the everlasting arms."

The following Monday, February 10, 1947, Mair passed away to be with her Lord. Just before breathing her last, she said : " The Lord answers prayer. Jesus ! Jesus ! Jesus !"

Mrs. Williams was now ill, and was ordered to be kept very quiet. Learning, however, that her husband was grieving, she went to his side, promising him she would not leave him again.

On February 13, in the early morning, she noticed a change
in his condition and sent for the doctor. A few hours later,
he passed into the presence of his Lord. His last words were :
" I shall be satisfied when I awake with His likeness. Leave
me now to God and to peace." Mrs. Williams immediately
thanked the Lord for the twenty-nine years she had had with
her husband. But now she was a widow. What she had
feared had come upon her. She opened her Bible, and asked
the Lord to give her a message. She was led to Hosea
2 : 16 : " It shall be at that day, saith the Lord, that thou
shall call me Ishi." The latter word in the margin means :
" My Husband." Thus she was comforted in her spirit.

On the day of the funeral the snow-clad fields leading
from Penygroes village to " Glanyrafon " house formed an
appropriate setting for the occasion. Many friends of the
deceased and his family wended their way to the house for
the service there at 2 p.m. on Tuesday, February 18, 1947.
Not only had they, a believing company, been made white
in the blood of the Lamb, but he who was their beloved
apostle, had departed to be with his Lord, and was in the
celestial realm, walking with Christ in white.

Pastor Dan, as he had been affectionately known, had
asked that those who had been with him in the early days
should take part in the funeral service, so Pastor W. H.
Lewis was asked to act as Chairman. At " Glanyrafon "
the President's widow, kept prayerfully calm, a real princess
in Israel, and the family and relatives were resigned to God's
will. At the house Pastor Isaac Martin, Scotland, read the
comforting promises of John 14. The Rev. Lumley Williams,
Tenby, a son of the late Pastor J. J. Williams, the President's
uncle, offered prayer and thanksgiving for the example and
powerful spiritual ministrations of his deceased cousin, while
afterwards the large company outside sang a song of praise
to God, in words of the deceased's own composition. After

that a very large company marched slowly to the Apostolic Temple, but the great building was too small to accommodate the crowd.

After an opening hymn Pastor T. Rees expressed thanks to God in prayer for the gift of shining brilliance whom the Head of the Church had bestowed upon His Church. Pastor W. H. Lewis, the chairman, next spoke, and it is worthwhile repeating his opening remarks. " Very rarely do we hear of two funerals taking place in one home during the one week, father and daughter being carried to their last resting place within five days of each other, and the mother, herself, ill in bed and suffering. Our hearts go out today in prayerful sympathy with her, and to the whole family in this hour of trial and sorrow that has befallen them. Another thing that makes this historic gathering noteworthy is that we are laying to rest the mortal remains of the Founder and first President of the Apostolic Church."

Pastors V. Wellings, H. V. Chanter, W. M. Humphreys, D. T. Rennie, J. O. Jones, N. P. Jensen, Denmark, the Rev. Berian James, representing denominational ministers on the platform, and Pastor Gwilym Francis, representing the Bible Pattern Fellowship, paid tribute to the faithfulness, the courage, the loyalty and unfailing love for His Master that characterized so strongly the life of Pastor D. P. Williams. They also expressed their sympathy to the relatives. Afterwards Pastor T. V. Lewis delivered a message from Eccles. 12 : 7 and II Tim. 4 : 7, 8.

Cables and telegrams were read from the Missionary Centre, Bradford, Calabar missionaries, Norway, Australia, Canada, Denmark and U.S.A. Other telegrams came from friends in the homeland, including Pastor George Jeffreys, Bible Pattern Fellowship, Pastor Donald Gee, Assemblies of God, and Pastor Ben Griffiths, Peniel, London.

All present knew that the Church had suffered a great loss,

for as of old a prince and a great man had fallen in Israel.
Pastor D. P. Williams was a man greatly beloved, and he was
dominated by the Apostolic Vision, labouring in and out of
season for it. A fitting sentiment was expressed in a verse
recited at the service :

" Had he asked us, well we know, we should cry,
    ' O, spare the blow,'
And with streaming tears would say : ' Lord, we
    love him, let him stay.'

But the Lord doth nought amiss, and since He
    hath ordered this,
We have naught to do, but still, rest in silence on
    His will."

Finally, Pastor T. Davies, familiarly known as "The Scribe,"
who had been associated with the Pastor as literary assistant
for twenty-seven years, concluded with prayer. At the grave-
side, Pastor C. C. Ireson, London, read the committal lines
and II Cor. 1 : 10. The large crowd sang the closing hymn,
and the concluding prayer and benediction were offered by
Pastor T. V. Lewis.

On Monday afternoon of the August 1948, Penygroes
International Convention, the marble memorial over the
grave of Pastor D. P. Williams was unveiled. In spite of
heavy rain a goodly crowd attended the ceremony. After
the singing of a hymn and the offering of a prayer by Pastor
W. Phillip, Pastor T. V. Lewis, then President of the General
Council, gave an opening Word, followed by the unveiling
of the memorial by Mrs. D. P. Williams. Other speakers
were Pastors John Lindsay, H. V. Chanter, John Cardwell,
Thomas Rees, N. P. Jensen and H. Cousen. All gave to
God praise and thanks for the exemplary devotion of Pastor
D. P. Williams. A hymn and prayer closed the ceremony.

Truly Daniel Powell Williams and William Jones Williams were great gifts of God to His Church. They are no longer with us, but they still speak to us, inspiringly. We can show our appreciation of all they did and sacrificed by giving to the Lord Jesus Christ a devotion and love like theirs.

We look forward to the day that we shall meet them again at our Lord's Return. The Christian religion is one of glorious expectation, an expectation of being together in heaven with Christ and with His saints. Our home is not on earth, but in heaven. Here we are pilgrims and strangers : heaven is our abiding-place. There we shall have the joy of meeting our beloved in Christ who have gone before, and the holy angels, and have fellowship with them, and above all with the Father, the Son and the Holy Spirit.